GOLF®
MAGAZINE

The Best
Instruction
Guide Ever!

The Ultimate Guide to Improving Your Game and Shooting Lower Scores

From the Top 100 Teachers in America

EDITED BY DAVID DENUNZIO

Time Inc.
HOME ENTERTAINMENT

Time Inc.
1271 Avenue of the Americas
New York, New York 10020

If you would like to order any of
our hardcover Collector's
Edition books, please call us at
(800) 327-6388.
(Monday through Friday,
7:00 a.m. - 8:00 p.m. or
Saturday, 7:00 a.m. - 6:00 p.m.
Central Time)

Design by Paul Ewen
Cover photographs by
Bob Atkins and Angus Murray

YOUR BEST GOLF EVER!

Despite any success you've had in the past, the guide in your hands is going to help you shoot lower scores and better enjoy your golfing experience. Confident claims no doubt, but they're easily made considering the source of the hundreds of tips, drills and lessons contained within. Each one comes straight out of the pages of *GOLF Magazine*, the most widely read golf publication in the world. With an almost 50-year legacy of award-winning instruction, *GOLF* has become the leader in the way the game is taught and played. Moreover, its instruction is driven by the single greatest collection of teaching experts in the game: the Top 100 Teachers. Members of this elite group are chosen not only for their swing knowledge and experience, but also for their teaching skills and knack for developing methods that make the game easier to learn. Some of the Top 100 Teachers you know by name—the ones that work with the major stars on the professional tours. Others are teaching legends with hall-of-fame status. But all of them are dedicated to helping golfers just like you get better and making sure these changes stick.

Since their debut in 1996, the Top 100 Teachers have produced more than 3,000 pages of instruction in *GOLF Magazine*. This guide represents their greatest hits, organized to build your game from the ground up the right way. Use their advice to hit the ball farther, putt better and beat anything the course throws at you. With the help of the Top 100 Teachers, your best golf ever is just around the corner.

DAVID DeNUNZIO, INSTRUCTION EDITOR, *GOLF MAGAZINE*

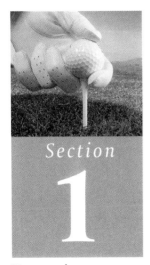

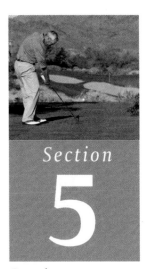
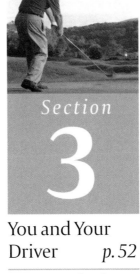
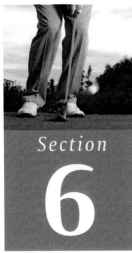
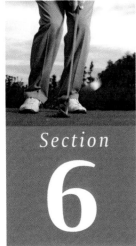

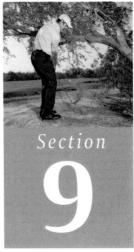

A quick look at the nation's most exclusive—and talented—team of teaching experts.

GOLF
MAGAZINE
TOP
100
TEACHERS
IN AMERICA

What you do before your rounds and the time spent between them determines the scores you shoot and how quickly you can lower them.

SECTION 1

PREPARING TO PLAY

How to get your round motoring out of the blocks even before you hit your first shot

There are two parts to the game: the playing part and the part that occurs between rounds. While your time on the course lasts about four hours, the time from the moment you putt out on 18 to when you place your tee in the ground on the first hole of your next round is significantly longer. For some golfers, weeks longer. And although you judge your game by the scores you shoot, it's really what you do between rounds—and just before you tee off—that determines the numbers you mark on your card.

The fact that you're holding this book in your hands means you're serious about your game and about improving. The majority of these pages are dedicated to helping you get around the course in the fewest strokes possible. This section, however, focuses on what you need to do between rounds to make sure the lessons stick. With the help of the Top 100 Teachers, you'll learn how to warm up before play to get off to good starts, how to make your practice time serious learning time, how to select the gear that will help you save strokes and how to make your lessons more effective. Armed with this knowledge, you'll optimize the non-playing part of your game so you can put your swing on autopilot and shoot the scores you want.

5 THINGS YOU'LL LEARN IN THIS SECTION

- How to get your swing warm before you play, whether you have an hour to get ready or just 15 minutes
- How to shop for equipment and secure the right mix of clubs to help you score low
- How to select a teacher and get the most out of a lesson
- How to practice with a purpose, make effective practice swings and groove the right moves quickly
- The flaw you must fix first

YOUR GAME

How to be a "Player"

Here are three tricks that only pros know

● Play with the right ball. Most golfers don't know what that is. As a general rule, choose the ball that works best for you when putting and chipping, not the one you can hit the farthest.
—**Bruce Patterson**

● Learn to adapt to different weather conditions with your gear. For instance, if it's cold, use a driver with a lower loft and move the ball a bit back in your stance. When the weather turns, the optimum launch angle isn't 12 degrees. It's more like 8 degrees.
—**Peter Krause**

● You've probably been told to finish your swing with your hands high. But if you want to hit the ball farther, consider finishing low. Watch the big hitters on the pro tours—the club comes to rest on their left shoulder. This is the result of unhinging the wrists fully through impact. It provides a powerful snap to the swing and produces a low finish.
—**Mike Lopuszynski**

WARM UP AND PRACTICE

How to get loose before play and keep your swing skills fresh between rounds

The 15-Minute Warm-Up

A quick and effective routine to jump-start your round

The situation

You've arrived late to the course and have only 15 minutes to warm up.

The solution

Get your short game and putting warm because you'll need them more than ever while you work out the kinks in your full swing.

What to do

This plan calls for six two-minute segments and allows for three minutes to pick up balls and move between drills. First, stretch your hamstring muscles and twist your trunk all the way right and left to loosen up a bit.

Step 1

Take five swings each with your 7-iron, 5-wood and driver at 3/4 speed. Don't hit balls, just swing the clubs.

Step 2

Grab three balls and your 8-iron, 60-degree wedge and putter, and hightail it for the practice green.

Step 3

Hit the short-game shots described at right in order. If you can squeeze in one full swing before you tee off, hit a 4-wood out onto the range. You'll be ready to start your round with a smooth 4-wood into the first fairway.

—Dave Pelz

Hit three lofted pitch shots over a practice bunker with your lob wedge (or highest-lofted club) to learn how the ball reacts upon hitting the green.

Jump into the bunker and hit three short sand shots to a greenside target to activate your hands.

Hit three running chips with your 8-iron to a hole 50 feet away to get a feel for distance.

Stroke three extra-long lag putts well across the putting surface to dial in the speed of the greens.

Hit six three-foot putts to become comfortable with the short ones—these are the score-breakers.

INSTRUCTION
Start With Your Short Game

Most golfers warm up with their longer clubs first. This is why they start their rounds poorly.

Statistical averages show golfers score better on the middle 10 holes than the first and last four. It's easy to see how the pressure to shoot a certain score might make you nervous and result in poor scores at the finish. But poor play on the first four holes? Perhaps this is because you're not prepared to scramble when you miss the first few greens. This data emphasizes the importance of warming up your short-game feel and touch before heading to the first tee. A complete-game warm-up is optimal, but when you're short on time, warm up your scoring game first!
—**Dave Pelz**

Golfers score better on the middle holes than early or late. Warm up your short game first to buck this trend.

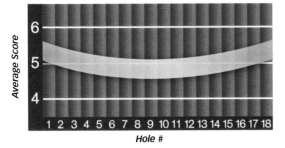

How to Customize Your Warm-Up
Find the pre-round prep that works best for you

On Tour, I notice that some players take just 40 minutes to get ready, while others warm up for several hours. My point is this: Your pre-round preparation must be tailored to your personality and body conditioning. What gets one player ready to play their best may tire you out. Optimize your scoring potential by trying different warm-up times and techniques, and keeping track of the scores you shoot afterward. Once you learn what works best for you, use it for all of your rounds in the future.
—**Dave Pelz**

DRILL
How to Loosen Up Your Body
Follow these steps for peak performance

Whether your pre-round warm-up time is an hour (ideal) or 15 minutes (typical), you have time to get ready for one of your best rounds. Here's the sequence to follow:

Step 1
Walk briskly to the driving range to get your blood moving, then warm up. Hold two clubs together and swing them in circles, doing 10 reps with each arm. This prepares your shoulders for the demands of the swing.

Step 2
Rest the clubs on the ground and hold them vertically, securing your hands on both grips [above]. Keep your hands there and do 10 squats to warm up your knees, calves and hips.

Step 3
Hit your short irons for a solid 10 minutes. Start with slow, three-quarter length swings and gradually build to full swings. After 10 minutes of hitting balls you can stretch your arm, leg and core muscles however you like without risking a visit to the chiropractor the next day.
  Even if you don't hit another ball after this last step, your body will be primed to hit a good drive on the first tee and sustain high performance throughout your round.
—**Dave Phillips**

How to Practice Like a Tour Player

Improve your rhythm—and look cool doing it!

START HERE
Tip over a bucket of balls and, with your club in your right hand, pull a ball out of the pile and drag it over to a spot where you can hit it.

The problem
You go through a bucket of range balls like a wave of locusts through a cornfield.

The solution
When you beat balls at a machine-gun pace you're not helping your game much. You need to set up to the ball correctly every time, and also take the time to follow through completely, study your ballflight and landing patterns, and then decompress and get ready for the next shot. In other words, you need to practice like you play.

How to do it
Watch Tour players on the driving range. Most pros follow a six-step procedure that takes them from ball to ball in a deliberate, measured way that mimics how they approach each shot on the golf course. If you copy that procedure, you're guaranteed to become a better ball striker.
—John Elliott, Jr.

Now "Present" the handle of the club to your right hand, release your left hand, and go back to Step 1. Now you're practicing like a pro!

Stand behind your ball and pick your target. Step into address—first with your right foot and then with your left— while glancing at your target.

As the ball comes to a stop, remove your right hand from the grip and allow the club to slide down the fingers of your left hand until it feels light and balanced in your hand.

Make a complete, balanced swing so that you're facing the target and most of your weight is on your left foot. Study the flight of your ball, and stay in this position until it has landed.

Once you're comfortable in your address position and have visualized your target line, waggle the club once or twice to loosen your wrists, and then swing away.

How to Practice Your Putting

Six tips for making your time on the practice green pay off

SAVE TRICK SHOTS FOR POOL
It might be fun to slide a 60-foot putt through a slalom course of tees, but on the course you're more likely to miss the straight 3-footers.

PLAY FOR KEEPS
Have a nine-hole putting contest with a buddy. This is the best way to prepare for a match. You'll be forced to make putts under competitive pressure, just as you will on the course.

NEVER GIVE AN INCH
Ever laugh at a guy practicing 1-foot putts and then lose to him? Practice some short ones. You'll win more matches by assuming you'll never be conceded a putt.

DON'T BE A DRONE
Don't repeatedly drain the same well-trodden putt, as if every one you face will be a 6-footer with the same right-to-left break. Practice putts that vary in length and slope to more accurately match the putts in a typical round.

TALK IS CHEAP
Don't look at the practice green only as a place to unload a new batch of jokes. If you take putting practice seriously, your results will speak for themselves.

SET GOALS
Try to make 10 3-footers in a row along a tee- or coin-marked wheel around the cup. If you miss on No. 9, start over. Then try three in a row from 10 feet. Goal-setting breeds discipline and confidence.
—Gale Peterson

Practice These Major Keys

Other than working on technique, what should I focus on during my practice sessions?

"Practice with the club that allows you to hit the fairway on the most consistent basis, even if it's a 3-wood. Don't feel like your driver is the only club you can hit from the tee box. Also, work on shots around the green, particularly on putts from four feet and in. I've seen it help players drop three strokes in three days."
—Rod Lidenberg

"Hit little punch shots with your 7-iron to ingrain the feel of a correct release. Address a ball, and cock the club up so the club shaft is parallel to the ground. Hold it there, get comfortable and start the swing from this point, taking your hands back to chest height. Start down with your hips and finish at chest height. This drill trains your hands and arms to store the power of the downswing for as long as possible."
—Ron Gring

"Hit shots with the sole purpose of maintaining your posture from start to finish. You can practice this at home, too. Place a pillow against a wall and rest your forehead against it, then make practice takeaways without moving your head off the pillow."
—Gerald McCullagh

TO GET THE RIGHT GEAR

Even if your swing is sound, it won't do you much good if you're playing with the wrong equipment. Here's how to round out your perfect set.

How to Shop Smart

Eight ways to gear up and find value, fit and quality

FLY SOLO
Go alone and let the salesman help you make decisions. Many golfers end up making bad purchases based on advice from a buddy who knows very little about equipment.

CAP YOUR WALLET
Follow a budget to prevent buyer's remorse. Set a price range for the final bill rather than for each individual item. This will give you the flexibility to spend more money on one thing and less on another.

STEP IN IT
Make sure a shoe is comfortable right out of the box. It's not going to fit any better on the course. Also look for a lighter athletic or sneaker-type shoe if you prefer to walk more than you take a cart.

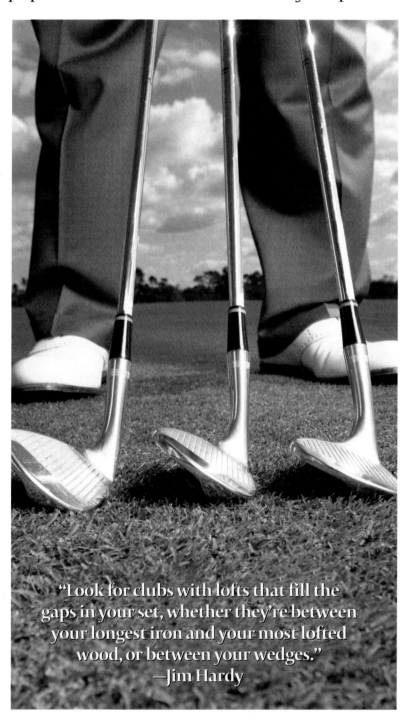

"Look for clubs with lofts that fill the gaps in your set, whether they're between your longest iron and your most lofted wood, or between your wedges."
—Jim Hardy

SUIT UP
Reach for synthetic fabrics that wick away moisture and prevent wrinkles. You'll get the most value from neutral colors—they mix and match the easiest.

IRON OUT YOUR BAG
The average golfer needs more hybrids and fewer long irons. Once the salesman knows what type of courses you play, he can tell you what ratio of irons to wedges to hybrids you need.

TEST YOUR EYES
Good sunglasses will have no distortion when you look at the ground through the bottom of the lenses. Take a pair outside for a two-minute test—if they darken up and take the glare out of the parking lot, they're keepers.

GET FIT
A fitting for woods, irons, a driver, grip size and balls takes at most 30 minutes. Most stores have a launch monitor or a simulator so the salesman can fit you and then recommend clubs for your game.

TELL THE TRUTH
Be honest about how you hit the ball, how you strategize and what clubs you favor. Telling the truth about your game is the only way to get a proper fit.

How to Find the Right Mix of Clubs

Follow these rules and you'll always have the right club for the shots you typically face during play

Player's Bag	**Low-Handicapper's Bag**	**Mid-Handicapper's Bag**	**High-Handicapper's Bag**
These specs should suit you if you carry your 5-iron 170-190 yards and your driver 250-275 yards.	These specs should suit you if you carry a 5-iron 155-170 yards and your driver 230-250 yards.	These specs should suit you if you carry a 5-iron 150-160 yards and your driver 220-235 yards.	These specs should suit you if you carry a 5-iron 130-140 yards and your driver 205-220 yards.
SHAFTS	**SHAFTS**	**SHAFTS**	**SHAFTS**
Irons: Steel, stiff flex **Woods:** Graphite, stiff or extra stiff	**Irons:** Steel, stiff flex **Woods:** Graphite, stiff flex	**Irons:** Graphite, regular or stiff flex **Woods:** Graphite, reg or stiff	**Irons:** Graphite, regular flex **Woods:** Graphite, regular flex
SET	**SET**	**SET**	**SET**
Irons: Hybrid driving iron, 4-iron to PW, Gap, SW, LW **Woods:** Driver, Strong 3-wood	**Irons:** Hybrid, 4-iron to PW, Gap, SW, LW **Woods:** Driver, 4-wood	**Irons:** Hybrid, 5-iron to PW, Gap, SW **Woods:** Driver, 3-, 5- and 7-wood	**Irons:** Three hybrids, 6-iron to PW, Gap, SW, LW **Woods:** High-lofted driver, 4-wood
BALL	**BALL**	**BALL**	**BALL**
Multilayer, urethane-covered model (favoring spin)	Multilayer, urethane-covered model (favoring distance)	Three-piece performance (distance/spin blend)	Low-compression distance

YOUR KEY CLUB	**YOUR KEY CLUB**	**YOUR KEY CLUB**	**YOUR KEY CLUB**
Strong 3-wood	**Lob wedge**	**Gap wedge**	**Hybrids**
With your length, you won't need to pull driver on every tee, especially on short or troublesome par 4s. More fairways mean more birdies.	You've established a decent long game. Now it's time to learn to save shots around the greens. The Lob wedge is a savior from deep bunkers and dense rough.	Mastering this club will allow you to take full swings on finesse shots from 100 yards in, a spot you'll encounter since you likely lose some carry on full shots.	Lose the long irons and launch the type of high, soaring shots you see more accomplished players hit. The versatile hybrid is also useful around the greens.

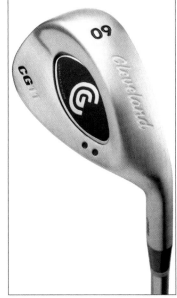

"Try one hybrid at a time so you can adjust to the club and see what it can do."
—Ed Ibarguen

HOW TO LEARN

You can do it yourself and take years to get better. Or you can seek out a qualified teaching professional and improve faster than you imagined.

CHECKPOINT

How to Get the Most From a Lesson

Six ways to get what you pay for— a better game

CHOOSE YOUR CLASSROOM
Decide whether you need a range lesson or a playing lesson. If you're looking to improve your swing and ball striking, the range is the best place. But if you want better course management, take a playing lesson.

SET EXPECTATIONS
Before the lesson, tell your instructor what you're looking to improve and how much you'd like to accomplish. Don't expect to drop 10 strokes after one lesson and don't expect 300-yard drives if you're just learning to grip the club.

FIND THE RIGHT PRO
Ask your pals for suggestions, or check our teacher lists on golf.com. Call the pros and interview them. Ask them about their teaching style—what you can expect— then pick a teacher who appeals to your needs.

HIT REWIND
Start every practice session with a review of what you've been taught. Start with the basics then go through your last lesson. Don't abandon the teachings if you're not getting perfect results— keep at it and you'll start to see the payoff.

COOL DOWN
Spend another 15 minutes on the range after your lesson. Work on your own to relax and apply what you've just learned from your teacher. Also, take notes, and if your pro tapes the lesson, taking home a video is even better.

DON'T RUSH
Whether you're coming from home or the office, don't blaze into the parking lot and quickly throw on your spikes. To get your mind and body in optimal condition, arrive at your lesson 15 minutes early to loosen up.
—Rick McCord

CHECKPOINT

What You Need to Fix the Most

During lessons, practice and play, correct your most common flaws first. For most golfers, it's a slice.

The problem

Baseball, apple pie and left-to-right shots that defy the laws of physics—no doubt we are a country of slicers. But has America's slice-itis reached epidemic proportions?

A recent poll of the Top 100 Teachers offers hope. According to the Top 100, the slicing problem is improving—but thanks only to gear advances. While it's impossible to gauge technology's effect on accuracy, it's safe to say that our country is slicing less, but we're still a far cry from straight down the middle. We're left just as much as we are right, further proving that correcting your swing path is priority No. 1.

Who slices most?

None of the low-handicap golfers in our poll hit a slice, and 90% of the slices were hit by those with an index of 10 or higher.

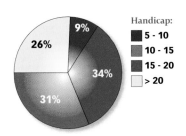

Handicap:
- ■ 5 - 10
- ▨ 10 - 15
- ▨ 15 - 20
- ☐ > 20

Where the shots went

A solid 25% of all shots flew straight. But 43% were either pulled or sliced? We've got some path fixin' to do!

Shot Type:
- ▨ Hook
- ■ Pull
- ▨ Push
- ▨ Slice
- ☐ Straight
- ▨ Topped/Fat

The experiment

We asked the starter at 69 courses managed by Troon Golf (*www.troongolf.com*) to report on the ball flights of the 9 a.m. foursome on Saturday, Sept. 2, 2006.

The results

More than 70 percent of the 276 tee shots measured failed to fly straight, with more than 38 percent finding the right side. Not exactly "Slice Saturday," but pretty close.

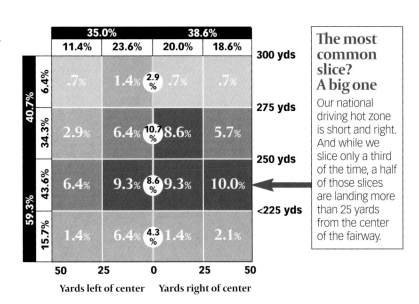

The most common slice? A big one

Our national driving hot zone is short and right. And while we slice only a third of the time, a half of those slices are landing more than 25 yards from the center of the fairway.

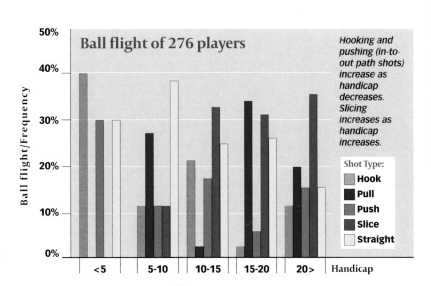

Ball flight of 276 players

Hooking and pushing (in-to-out path shots) increase as handicap decreases. Slicing increases as handicap increases.

Shot Type:
- ▨ Hook
- ■ Pull
- ▨ Push
- ▨ Slice
- ☐ Straight

Elite golfers base their swings on the principle that good positions lead to better positions in the segments of the swing that follow. Do likewise and the lasting improvement you're looking for will come more easily and more quickly than you expect.

SECTION 2

UNDERSTANDING YOUR SWING

How to make it simple and repeatable for consistent success

T he swing is a complex beast. This statement is no surprise to anyone who has tried to build one. Those that excel at it are the ones who commit to constant practice and study to turn the complexities into simple, repeatable actions. Unfortunately, you can't simply learn a swing and expect it to take your game where you want it to go. You must *understand* it. Only when you grasp how your setup and every motion affects what happens next in your swing will you truly be able to hit effective shots, stop bad ones when they occur and own the ability to self-correct and improve.

Like most instruction guides, this one starts at the beginning with your address. But unlike the rest, the Top 100 Teachers break down every facet of the swing that follows and provide insights and checkpoints you can use to improve every inch of your motion. It's a simple approach because correcting even just a few positions—or learning how to get into them correctly for the first time—automatically improves the positions that follow.

Follow this guide and you'll quickly become a true student of your swing and learn to recognize breakdowns in your technique. That's when the game you want will begin to take shape.

5 THINGS YOU'LL LEARN IN THIS SECTION

- **How to stand at address and hold the club correctly so it can swing itself**
- **How to swing on the proper plane and make powerful contact on the sweet spot**
- **Myths to avoid and swing secrets every golfer should know to hit successful shots**
- **Expert drills to turn your practice time into quality learning time**
- **A checkpoint at each moment of the swing to make sure you're doing it correctly**

Can You Really Get Better?

The Top 100 Teachers say YES! Over 90 percent of them reported you can drop your handicap by a third in three months. The exact way to accomplish this, however, varies.

LESSONS
At least one lesson a week: 60%

More than one lesson a week: 40%

PRACTICE
6 hours of practice a week: 48%

4 hours of practice a week: 22%   **More than 6 hours of practice a week: 30%**

"Practice six hours a week—four of those hours dedicated to the short game and the other two to tee shots. You'll shoot much lower scores if you can hit the fairway more often and get the ball close from short range."
—**Dr. David Wright**

"Regardless of your practice structure, use the following rule of thumb: 60 repetitions for each new motor skill learned, repeated for 21 days in a row."
—**Dr. T.J. Tomasi**

THE FIRST STEP

A fundamentally solid grip allows
you to make a natural motion
and stops swing errors in
their tracks

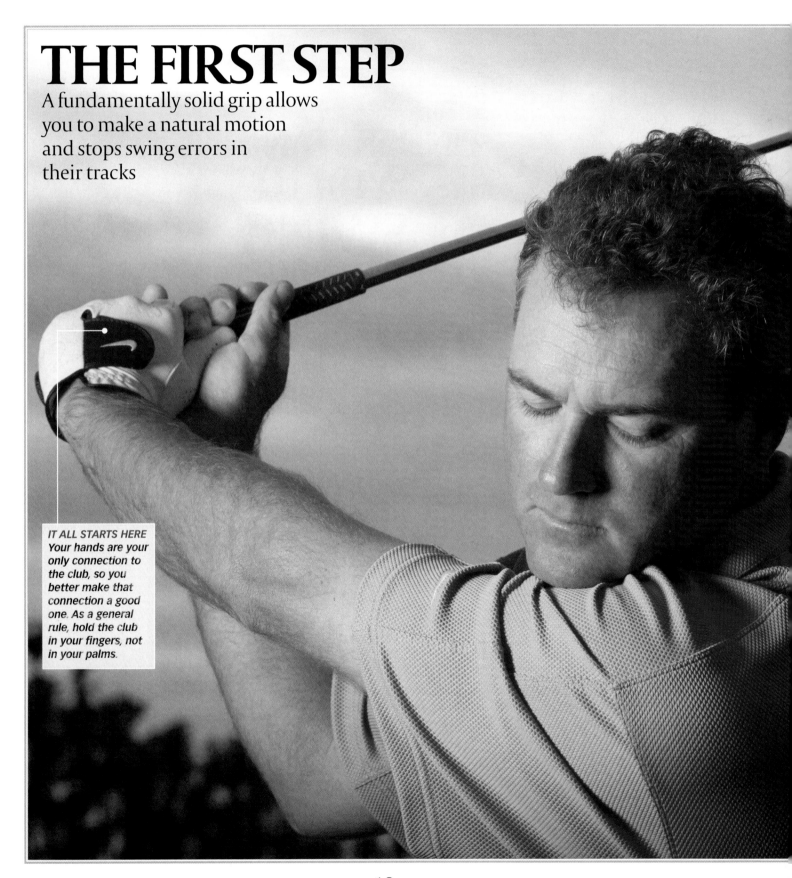

IT ALL STARTS HERE
*Your hands are your
only connection to
the club, so you
better make that
connection a good
one. As a general
rule, hold the club
in your fingers, not
in your palms.*

How to Grip Your Club

Use the creases in your hands to guide you into the perfect hold

Step 1
Do this without a glove to really get the feel of how to grip your clubs properly. Hold the handle against your outstretched left hand. The grip should extend diagonally from the fatty portion of your hand (just below the pinkie) to the middle crease of your index finger.

Step 2
Put your glove on and place the club how you had it in Step 1. Then, curl your fingers around the handle so that the fatty portion of your hand is on top. You should apply pressure with the last three fingers of your left hand. (You shouldn't feel any pressure in your palm.)

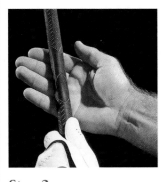

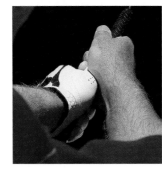

Step 3
When you position your right hand, the handle should rest across the base of your right pinkie to the top crease in your index finger. This ensures that you grip the club with your fingers, not your palm. Wrap your fingers around the underside of the grip and place the fatty portion of your right hand on top of your left thumb.

Step 4
Hold your grip out in front of you and check that the Vs formed by your thumbs and forefingers point to the right side of your face. Depending on your preference, rest your right pinkie in the crease between your left index and middle fingers (overlap grip) or wedge it between them (interlock).

—Brian Mogg

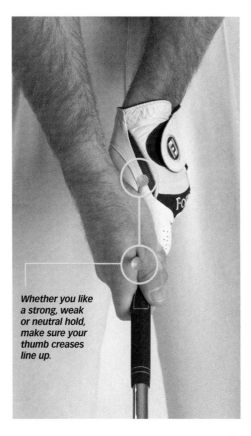

Whether you like a strong, weak or neutral hold, make sure your thumb creases line up.

Do Your Hands Work Together?

A lot of golfers can't hit the ball squarely because their hands work against each other, not with each other. To make sure that doesn't happen to you, take the following test.

● Grip any club and have a friend insert two tees in the creases formed by the base of your thumbs and the back of your hands as shown above. If one tee points to the right of your grip and the other points to the left, you've created opposing forces in your hands and you'll limit their ability to square up your clubface and release the club with authority.

● Your goal is to position your hands on the handle so that the two tees line up. In this position your hands can work as a single unit and deliver the club with maximum energy.

● If you slice, line up the tees over the right side of the grip. This gives you more power to square up the clubface through impact. Line the tees up over the left side of the grip to keep the face from closing too quickly and reel in your hook.

—Jason Carbone

How Much Squeeze Do I Need?

"I recommend that you grip the club as though you were gluing your hands to it. You want complete contact. Every bit of the insides of your fingers should be touching the handle. No gaps, no air pockets and no spaces."
— Bob Toski

"Hold your club over your right shoulder and pretend to throw it end over end without letting go of the club. The feeling you have when holding your club and going through the throwing motion is a good fit for your grip and grip pressure."
—Craig Harmon

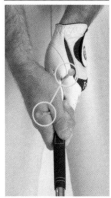

You'll suffer from a lack of distance and control with a misaligned grip.

SETUP BASICS

The majority of your swing errors—and the need to make compensations—are the result of mistakes in your setup. Get it right here and your swing will take care of itself.

How to Step Into Your Shot

Here's a reliable way to get your stance width correct every time

Step 1
Aim your clubface at your target then step in with your right foot, pointing it behind the ball. This cue is a reminder that you're starting to position the ball. You might even repeat that objective to yourself ("inside left heel," "center of stance," etc.).

Step 2
With your right foot in place, step in with your left. Position it relative to where you want to play the ball. The above is a 5-iron, so the ball goes four inches inside your left heel. A driver, played off your left heel, would require a smaller step.

Step 3
Step out with your right foot, widening your stance until you feel comfortable and stable. With your stance and ball position set, take a quick final look at the target, then return your eyes to the ball and begin your swing.
—**Don Hurter**

Rock Your Feet to Find Your Balance

Balanced swings are good swings, and good balance starts at address.

Start by standing tall with your arms at your sides, then bend forward and flex your knees, like a linebacker ready to pounce in any direction. Keep your neck in line with your spine, and hinge so that  your hips remain over your heels and your arms dangle freely below your shoulders.

After you settle into the above position, rock gently forward on your toes, then back onto your heels and forward again so that your weight is evenly distributed across each foot. This simple drill places you in perfect balance and in position to make a controlled swing.
—**David Glenz**

How to Take Your Stance

Copy the positions below to build a rock-solid address position and set the stage for a successful swing

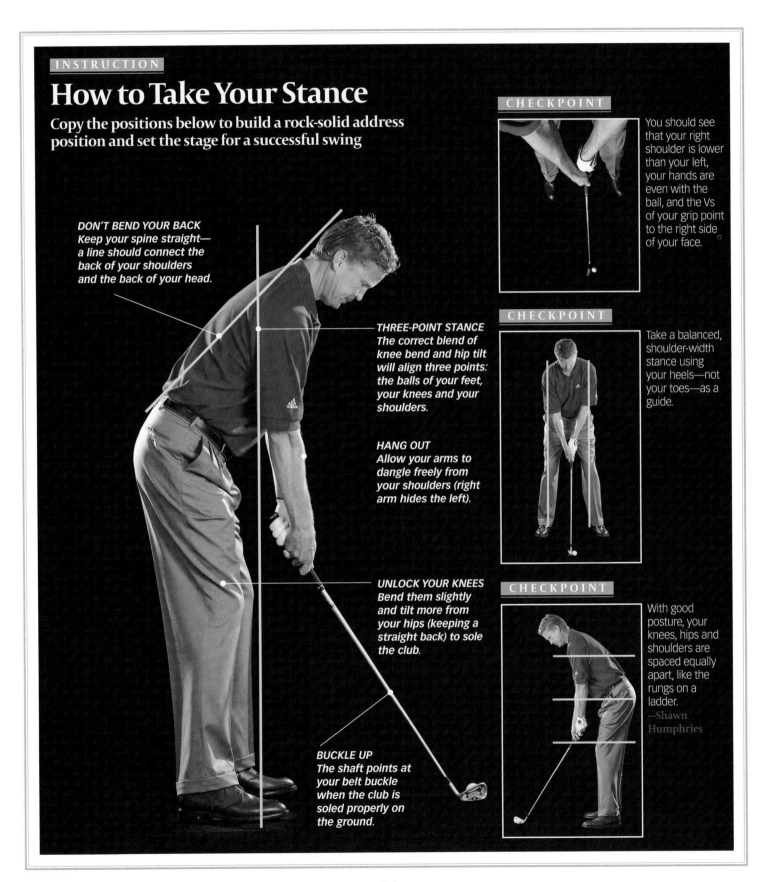

DON'T BEND YOUR BACK
Keep your spine straight—a line should connect the back of your shoulders and the back of your head.

THREE-POINT STANCE
The correct blend of knee bend and hip tilt will align three points: the balls of your feet, your knees and your shoulders.

HANG OUT
Allow your arms to dangle freely from your shoulders (right arm hides the left).

UNLOCK YOUR KNEES
Bend them slightly and tilt more from your hips (keeping a straight back) to sole the club.

BUCKLE UP
The shaft points at your belt buckle when the club is soled properly on the ground.

CHECKPOINT

You should see that your right shoulder is lower than your left, your hands are even with the ball, and the Vs of your grip point to the right side of your face.

CHECKPOINT

Take a balanced, shoulder-width stance using your heels—not your toes—as a guide.

CHECKPOINT

With good posture, your knees, hips and shoulders are spaced equally apart, like the rungs on a ladder.
—Shawn Humphries

Adjust Your Grip to Hit Straighter Shots

Experiment with different holds to find the one that works best

When you feel you're aimed correctly but your shots are missing left or right of your target, consider adjusting your grip. A grip that fails to complement your swing style can cause you to miss even if you make a solid effort. Experiment with the following grips and see if a change to either a weaker or stronger hold will help you hit more accurately.
—Kevin Walker

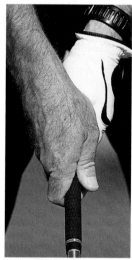

Weak Grip
Beats a hook
Hands on top of the handle, right V pointing to your nose.

How to Take Aim

Use close targets to prevent shots that fly off line

Step 1
Once you've decided on a target, pick out a divot or another obvious spot on the ground about a foot in front of your ball. The spot should sit on the line that runs from your ball to the target. Imagine a track that extends out from the entire clubhead, toe to heel *[inset photo]*. Thinking of it as a lane instead of a line makes it easier to check that you're aimed correctly.

Step 2
Once you have your aiming lane, hold your club steady and stand with your feet nearly touching. Position your feet so that the leading edge of the club is perpendicular to your toe line. Now you're set to produce a swing that travels on a plane that matches your line to the target. Widen your stance to address the ball and swing with confidence.
—Nancy Quarcelino

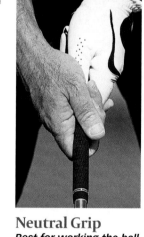

Neutral Grip
Best for working the ball
Hands slightly right on the handle, right V pointing to your right cheek bone.

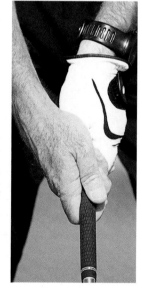

Strong Grip
Beats a slice
Hands resting on the right side of the handle, both Vs pointing to your right ear.

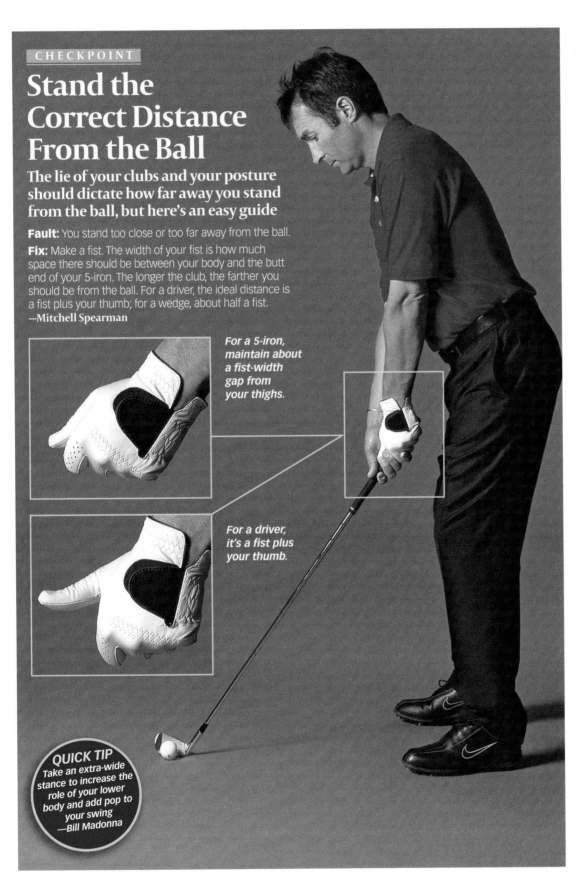

Stand the Correct Distance From the Ball

The lie of your clubs and your posture should dictate how far away you stand from the ball, but here's an easy guide

Fault: You stand too close or too far away from the ball.

Fix: Make a fist. The width of your fist is how much space there should be between your body and the butt end of your 5-iron. The longer the club, the farther you should be from the ball. For a driver, the ideal distance is a fist plus your thumb; for a wedge, about half a fist.
—Mitchell Spearman

For a 5-iron, maintain about a fist-width gap from your thighs.

For a driver, it's a fist plus your thumb.

QUICK TIP
Take an extra-wide stance to increase the role of your lower body and add pop to your swing
—Bill Madonna

Your Right Foot First

Here's another way to make sure you're aimed at your target

Step 1

Set the middle of your right foot perpendicular to your target line and even with the back edge of the ball with no knee flex. Set your left-hand grip.

Step 2

Place your club on the ground behind the ball without trying to aim the clubface. The shaft should line up with your left forearm. The clubface will look open, but don't change it.

Step 3

Add your right hand to the club and bring your left foot even with your right. Notice that your hips and shoulders are parallel to each other. Swivel your head, fix your eyes on your target and spread your feet into your regular stance width. When you look back down at the ball, your clubface will still look open. Again, don't change it—that's the adjustment you need to combat what's called "hidden offset" that results when the toe of your iron sits up at address. Trust it, and you'll hit more accurate shots, particularly with your short irons.
—Dr. David Wright

Pick the Right Ball Position

The trick? Know where your nose is.

Each club in your bag features a unique length and lie angle (the angle the shaft creates when the clubhead is soled on the ground). Because of this, you must vary where you play the ball in your stance to accommodate the dimensions of the club in your hands. As a general rule, the longer the club the more forward you should position the ball in your stance, but the ball should never be left of your left shoulder or right of your nose, regardless of which club you're using for full swings. This photo shows an easy way to remember exactly where to position the ball for every shot.

"You stand taller with a 3-iron than with a 7-iron, so it will bottom out later in your swing—that's why you play the ball forward in your stance with longer clubs."

Putter | PW-7 | 3-6 iron | Hybrid/ Fairway wood | Driver

Use Your Body to Position the Ball

Line up the ball correctly in your stance with this anatomical guide

Driver
Position the ball even with the outside of your left shoulder.

Hybrid/Woods
Position the ball even with the center of your left armpit.

3- to 6-iron
Position the ball even with your left ear for long and mid-irons.

Short irons
Play the ball off your left cheek for short irons and wedges.

Putter
Play the ball even with your nose to sink more putts.

Once you have your ball position set, make two final checks at address: your weight distribution and your shaft position.

Check 1
For standard full swings with every club, make sure your weight is evenly spread over both of your feet. This provides you with a stable platform to help you maintain balance throughout your motion.

Check 2
If you have difficulty making clean contact consistently, press the shaft slightly forward by moving your hands toward the target (be careful not to move the clubhead as well). This gives you the best chance for ball-first contact and solid strikes.

—**Michael Breed**

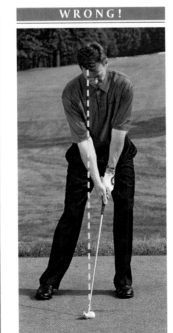

WRONG! WRONG!

The ball position in both photos is in exactly the same position, but my incorrect weight distribution in each photo changes the position of the ball in relation to my head. For the short iron I have here the ball should be positioned off my left cheek. This underlines the need for even weight distribution.

When Is It Time to Use a New Ball?

The modern ball is pretty durable and will hold its properties for a long time. **A top-tier ball will last for about three rounds and a lower quality ball will last slightly less.** Even if you hit down on the ball hard and hit a lot of bunkers and cart paths, the only damage you'll really see will be a duller finish. When the finish wears, your ballflight will be affected and replacing it wouldn't be a bad idea. However, most modern urethane covers make this a slow process and most golfers will lose the ball before serious wear occurs.

"If you're not hitting many greens in regulation, switch to a ball that's a bit softer to help you more with your short game."
—**Steve Bosdosh**

How High Should You Tee the Ball?

Our exclusive test provides the rock-solid answer

The Experiment

Twenty-seven golfers, aged 25 to 71 with handicaps ranging from scratch to 29, were divided into three groups of nine by handicap level: 0-9, 10-19, and 20 and above. Each golfer hit 10 drives at each tee height (low: top edge of ball even with top of clubhead; medium: equator of ball even with the top of the clubhead; and high: bottom of ball even with the top of the clubhead). Each group hit from the three tee heights in varying order to ensure that fatigue and motivation were balanced. Only the best five out of each player's 10 drives at each tee height were recorded so that mis-hits would not skew the data. Participants used their own drivers, with clubheads ranging from 410 cc to 460 cc.

The Analysis

Carry distance and other data were measured by a launch monitor. Accuracy also was recorded: drives that landed in the fairway were scored higher than those that landed in the rough or beyond the rough scored.

The Results

Carry distance for mid and high tee heights was significantly longer than the low tee height, largely an effect of the higher tees promoting higher launch angles and less spin. The high tee height provided the most distance, giving players an average of 12 yards more carry per drive than the low tee height.

—Eric Alpenfels

HANDICAP	Low tee	Mid tee	High tee
Low (0-9)			
Carry distance (yards)	211.64	219.62	222.92
Launch angle (degrees)	10.5	13.04	13.17
Ball spin (rpm)	4,051	3,875	3,434
Clubhead speed (mph)	98.32	97.08	97.36
Ball speed (mph)	138.59	138.13	138.95
Average carry: 218.06 yards			
Mid (10-19)			
Carry distance (yards)	171.46	177.84	179.84
Launch angle (degrees)	12.4	14.4	14.04
Ball spin (rpm)	3,844	3,794	3,529
Clubhead speed (mph)	86.04	85.76	85.24
Ball speed (mph)	120.9	120.93	120.93
Average carry: 176.38 yards			
High (20 and up)			
Carry distance (yards)	160.85	174.15	178.24
Launch angle (degrees)	11.23	13.7	14.75
Ball spin (rpm)	3,834	3,801	3,591
Clubhead speed (mph)	85.39	85.87	85.01
Ball speed (mph)	120.15	120.92	120.39
Average carry: 171.08 yards			

The perfect tee height—bottom of the ball at top of clubface. Tee your ball slightly above the crown.

INSTRUCTION

How to tee up for a...

Scoring iron
For a 6-iron through wedge, bury the tee in the ground so you can see only its head.

Long iron
For longer irons, leave about a ¼-inch of the tee above the ground.

Hybrid club
For hybrids and fairway woods, leave a ½-inch of the tee above the ground.

CHECKPOINT

The Moment of Impact
What happens when you do it right

Catching the ball on the beginning of the upswing produces a higher launch angle and less spin, leading to greater distance.

At impact, the ball compresses because of the force transferred to it from the clubhead. The ball actually sticks to the clubface, sliding and rolling on it for about .0004 seconds.

After impact, the ball leaves the clubface with whatever launch angle, speed and spin your swing has imparted to it. About 1 percent to 2 percent of deformation in the ball remains, causing tiny vibrations inside.

Once clear of the clubface, the vibrations are dampened out, and the ball is on its way.

Striking the ball above the center of the face—the new "sweet spot"—promotes a higher launch angle and less spin. These conditions result in a longer, more efficient ballflight that more than makes up for the clubhead rotation (and loss of ball speed) caused by hitting the ball above dead center.

WRONG!

Only half the ball is above the crown.

Results from the mid tee height came in second to the high tee height.

WRONG!

The entire ball is below the crown.

All three handicap groups lost distance on the low tee.

TAKEAWAY

Your hands start in a box...

BACKSWING

...and stay in the box during your takeaway.

Keep Your Hands "In the Box"

It's a key to getting your swing off to a good start

At address, notice how your hands fit nicely into a small rectangle *[above]*. This is your "hands box," and you'll know it's in the right place if you take your stance by bending from your hips so that the shaft is perpendicular to your spine. Make sure that your hands don't leave the box during your takeaway. If they move to the right of the box, you took your club back too far to the inside *[right]*.

—Michael Hebron

WRONG!

How to Turn Your Shoulders

Tilt as well as turn and get more yards

What you're told to do
Make a big shoulder turn to increase your power. However, testing indicates that turning your shoulders too much results in a flat shoulder plane. Flat shoulder turns don't deliver as much speed to the ball as those that are on plane.

What to do instead
Tilt your shoulders as well as turn them. The right amount of turn and tilt will position your shoulder line on the preferred plane line, helping you apply maximum force and speed to the ball.

How to know you're tilting correctly
Place your driver across the front of your shoulders and turn to the top of your backswing. Check the angle of the shaft after you've fully stretched your upper back muscles against your hips. If you've done it right, the shaft (and your shoulders) will point toward the ground slightly above the ball *[photo, below left]*. Now you're set for power and prepped to deliver all of it to the ball.

—Jon Tattersall

WRONG!

If the shaft looks horizontal then your shoulder turn is too flat and you'll hit a weak shot.

DRILL

How to Groove a Solid Backswing

Start your swing like a pro with these three drills

A bad backswing is often due to one of three things: a sway away from the target (causing a loss of power), a reverse pivot where you strand weight on your left leg (increasing the chance of a slice) or straightening your right leg (increasing the likelihood of thin contact). Each of these errors makes it nearly impossible to bring your club into the ball on the correct path, giving you little chance for a successful result. Before you spend hours bashing balls on the practice tee or invest your hard-earned money on the latest training aid, try these three drills. A shaft without a head on it can help you determine which problem is affecting your backswing and then show you how to correct it.—**Brian Mogg**

Fault: Swaying

Fix: Push the shaft into the ground outside your right leg, angled so that it touches your foot and leg up to your knee. Now take your normal backswing. If your right leg pushes the shaft back, you're swaying. Practice until you can turn without moving the shaft.

WRONG!

Fault: Reverse pivoting

Fix: Angle the shaft so that the grip touches your inner right thigh as shown. Now take your backswing. If your right leg pushes the shaft forward toward your front leg, you're reverse pivoting. Practice until you can turn without moving the shaft.

WRONG!

Fault: Losing right-knee flex

Fix: Position the shaft behind you so that the grip presses against the back of your right knee. If your right leg pushes the shaft upward into the back of your thigh on your backswing, you've lost your flex. The grip should remain behind your right knee.

WRONG!

INSTRUCTION

How to Hinge Your Wrists

Do it right and you'll produce power and accuracy

The problem
You know you're supposed to hinge your wrists, but you're not sure how to do it.

The solution
Use the image of a door hinge to guide each of your wrists in the right direction.

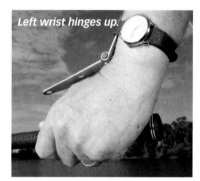

Left wrist hinges up.

Right wrist hinges back.

Your wrists hinge in two directions, either up-and-down or back-and-forth. During your takeaway, your left wrist should hinge up, not back. Picture a door hinge on top of your left forearm and thumb with the hinge rod at your wrist to remind you that your left wrist cocks up and down.

Your right wrist does the opposite— it should hinge back on your backswing and forward on your downswing. Imagine a door hinge on top of your wrist and forearm, with the hinge rod in the middle of your wrist. Use that as a guide to direct your right wrist cock both back and through.

During your backswing, picture hinges on both wrists and cock your left wrist up and your right wrist back. That sets your club on the correct backswing plane. If you hinge your right wrist up, your swing will be too steep; if you cock your left wrist back, your swing will get much too flat.
—**Martin Hall**

Correct hinge keeps your club on plane.

TOP 100 POLL

Q Should I think about hinging my wrists on my backswing, or should it happen naturally?

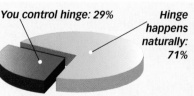

You control hinge: 29%

Hinge happens naturally: 71%

A "Your wrists can and will hinge in response to the momentum of the club, but if you grip the club too tightly that's not going to happen."
—**Scott Sackett**

INSTRUCTION

The One-Step Power Move

Make an "L" then move it up to achieve maximum width and power

At the end of your takeaway, rotate your forearms and hinge your wrists to create an L. Then, simply move the L to the top by turning your shoulders. This maintains the width of your swing and increases your power.
—**Shawn Humphries**

CHECKPOINT

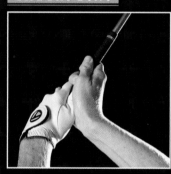

Your left wrist should be flat and your right wrist bent—the perfect anti-slice position.

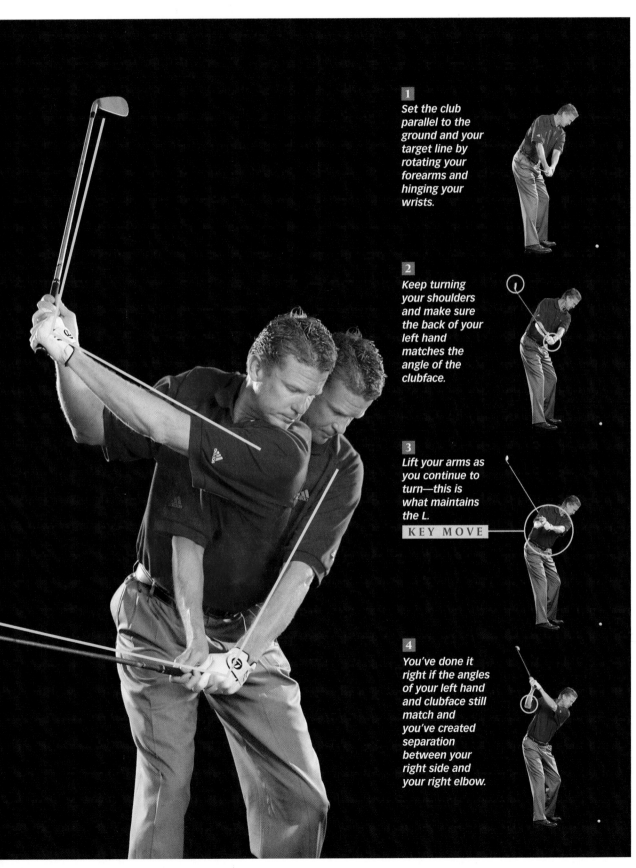

1

Set the club parallel to the ground and your target line by rotating your forearms and hinging your wrists.

2

Keep turning your shoulders and make sure the back of your left hand matches the angle of the clubface.

3

Lift your arms as you continue to turn—this is what maintains the L.

KEY MOVE

4

You've done it right if the angles of your left hand and clubface still match and you've created separation between your right side and your right elbow.

Carl Rabito
Turn, don't sway

"Take away the club with your right shoulder while keeping your chin and knees still. This will get your body properly behind the ball and eliminate swaying."

Keep your chin and knees quiet.

Brad Brewer
Smooth out your takeaway

"Your takeaway should be natural and free-flowing. Practice it by holding the club with only your thumbs and forefingers. This will keep you from whipping your club to the inside or swinging up too steeply."

A two-finger hold grooves a smooth takeaway.

Keep Your Tilt to Increase Your Coil

Here's how to power up behind the ball for big-time yards

Spine-tilt basics

In a fundamentally sound setup, your spine should tilt away from the target (to your right) about 5 degrees. This side bend is just as critical as your forward bend from your hips. If you're not bent to the right at address, you're bent left, and that's trouble.

How to tilt for power

As you swing to the top, increase your side bend by tilting your upper body to the right at least 10 degrees. A good way to think about it is to feel like you're moving the top of your spine farther away from the target than the bottom as you make your backswing turn. If you try to keep your spine constant in this sense—that is, don't tilt it to the right—you'll end up with a reverse pivot and a possible slice.

—Martin Hall

Increasing your side bend to the right on the backswing creates coil and stretch, and guards against a reverse pivot [inset].

WRONG!

Assume the power position: Spine tilted to right.

Peggy Kirk Bell
Watch your weight

"Don't allow your weight to get outside your right foot on your backswing. This inhibits the move back to your left side on your downswing. Make practice swings with a sand wedge placed under the outside of your right foot to remind you to keep your weight on the inside of your right foot."

Weight stays on the inside of your foot.

Roger Gunn
Use your shoulders as your guide

"Start your swing with your shoulders—they move your arms and your arms move the club. All of this happens around a steady head as your left shoulder turns under your chin."

Lead with your shoulders.

How to Control Your Turn

Use this simple drill to prevent overturning and destroying your backswing coil

Fault: You overturn on your backswing, making your downswing very difficult to control.

Fix: Stop your backswing at its natural stopping point. Try the drill at right to learn where that is. If you catch Tiger Woods during a practice round, you'll see him do this from time to time. This drill proves that your natural backswing length is determined by how far your can turn your left shoulder. If you feel you need more turn, get into the gym and start stretching.

—Bruce Hamilton

Get into your golf posture and address a ball. Take your left hand off the club and move your left arm under your right, placing the back of your left hand against your right elbow.

Take your backswing, keeping your left hand firmly against your right elbow the entire way to the top. Feel the muscles in your left shoulder stretch as you swing to the top.

When you can't turn any more, stop. Now you're loaded and in control. If you removed your left hand, you'd still be able to turn your right shoulder. That's overturn and it's bad for your game.

Swivel Your Head for Power

Keeping it still just cheats you of distance

The problem
You drive the ball straight, but not very far.

The solution
Move your left ear toward the ground during your backswing.

Why it works
When you try to keep your head still during your full swing, you restrict your ability to make a full turn. Swiveling your head, on the other hand, allows you to make a bigger shoulder turn, and that's a quick way to hit longer tee shots. Watch Tiger Woods when he swings. As he takes the club back, he moves his chin from left to right so that his left ear is closer to the ground at the top. Jack Nicklaus did the same thing, although he swiveled his head before he began his backswing. The key to this move is to keep it natural—allow your head to be carried along by your body turn.

—Brady Riggs

WRONG!
Keeping your head still blocks your upper body from turning as much as it can.

RIGHT!
Allowing your head to swivel with your body turn actually increases rotation and coil.

Get Square at the Top to Get Square at Impact

Dial in the correct face angle by bowing or flexing your left wrist

Slices, hooks and everything bad in between result from your clubface not squaring up to the ball at impact. This happens because you're not square at the top of your backswing, either. Good ball strikers know that if you're square to your path at the top (same clubface and shoulder angles), chances are you'll be square again at the bottom.

To check if you're doing it right, swing to the top and hold. If you're a slicer, the clubface is probably pointing at the target. **Try varying amounts of left and right wrist bend to match the face angle to your swing path.** Ultimately strive for a flat left wrist at the top of your swing. This will take care of what's happening at impact.

—Tim Mahoney

SQUARE

With very few exceptions, solid ball strikers have a flat left wrist position at the top.

OPEN

Adding left wrist cup opens the face and requires perfect timing to get square at impact.

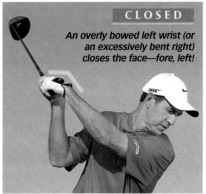

CLOSED

An overly bowed left wrist (or an excessively bent right) closes the face—fore, left!

DRILL

How to Stay on Plane Try the "hit the wall" drill

Fault: You turn your shoulders too aggressively to start your downswing and end up pulling the ball or hitting a wicked slice.

Fix: Take your address position with your back to a wall and swing your club to the top. With your clubhead barely touching the wall, bring your arms down to the mid-downswing position and stop. If you're guilty of turning your shoulders too hard, you'll notice you've lost contact with the wall *[far right photo]*. This drill helps you "slot" the club by sliding your left arm down and across your chest while keeping your club on plane.

—**Darrell Kestner**

Swing to the top...

...maintain contact...

...and never do this.

Pause for the amount of time it would take water to flow from the head to the grip before starting back down.

Pause at the Top for a Smoother Downswing

Patience leads to power

At address, imagine that your shaft is half-filled with water. Before you begin your swing, all of the water is in the bottom half of the shaft, but as you swing to the top gravity pulls the water toward the grip.

Instead of racing back down to the ball, allow the liquid to completely fill up the grip end of your shaft before you begin your downswing. **Just that little pause will keep you from lunging or lurching at the ball and make for an overall smoother motion.** Moreover, it will stop your hands from starting your downward motion and allow your lower body to lead and keep the correct downswing sequence—hips, shoulders, hands and clubhead—intact.

—Steve Bosdosh

How to Build Up "Lag Power"

Save your swing's energy for impact

Here's how to retain your right-hand angle so you don't release the cub too early and rob your swing of precious potential energy.

1 Stop.

Swing any club up to the top and stop. Check that your left shoulder has turned behind the ball with your weight over your right foot. Also, make sure that your left arm is firm and that your right arm is bent 90 degrees.

2 Stop.

Swing the club down until your left arm is parallel to the ground and stop. Make sure your right arm is still bent 90 degrees. Don't simply "pull the handle." This important first move down must come with a forward bump of weight.

3 Swing!

Straighten your right arm and fire your club through impact. Feel how the piston move puts outward pressure on the handle and keeps your wrists from losing their hinge. The only time both arms are straight is after impact.

—Kevin Walker

INSTRUCTION

How to Make a Solid Downswing

Keep it simple for sweet contact

Your goal should be to hit the sweet spot more consistently with every club in your bag. The best way for you to achieve it is to properly sequence your downswing. By that I mean following the four Hs: hips, handle, hands and (club)head. Thinking of your downswing in this order simplifies your thoughts, reduces the amount of effort you make, and produces more yards and purer strikes. The sequence of hips, handle, hands and clubhead is paramount for success. Here's how to get it.

CHECKPOINT

Your hips should stay in line with the tee.

1

Rotate your hips to start your swing

Stick a tee in the butt end of a 5-iron, hold it across your hips and get into your address position. The tee should point toward your target *[inset photo]*. Now shift onto your left leg, turning the tee to the left *[above]*—this is the motion your hips should take as you start your downswing motion.

CHECKPOINT

2

Lean the handle forward

The handle has to beat the clubhead to the ball in order to get powerful and consistent impact. Again, use your 5-iron with the tee in the grip. Swing to the top and, as you start down, immediately get the tee to point to the ground This will allow the grip to reach the ball first.
—**John Elliott, Jr.**

DRILL

Hit Correctly From the Inside

Trace an in-to-out path and you'll never slice again

Fault
You swing across the ball. Ideally, your clubhead should approach the ball on a path that's slightly inside of your target line.

Fix
Place three balls diagonally as shown and swing. Try to contact only the center ball. The only way to do this is to swing on an inside-out path. If you come over the top, you'll definitely hit the ball on the left, and maybe even all three balls. This drill works with every club in your bag.

Bonus
The "gate" created by the three balls is excellent for turning that slice-causing swipe into a draw.
—**Darrell Kestner**

Swing from the inside to kiss your slice goodbye.

Mike Bender
Lean the shaft forward

"This drill teaches you to make contact with a forward lean to the shaft. Draw a line in the sand down the middle of your stance. Using your left hand only, swing across the line, blasting out several divots in front of it. The object is to hit the sand and stop, so the grip stays ahead of the clubhead."

Lean the shaft forward.

Mike Davis
Don't collapse at the top

"Swinging your club past parallel doesn't mean extra power—it just means you're overswinging, usually because you collapse your wrists and left elbow at the top. To fix this, firm up your grip and try to keep your left arm straight. This doesn't shorten your swing—it strengthens it."

WRONG!
Folding your left elbow is a no-no.

RIGHT!
Keep your left arm straight.

Stay on plane with a tucked right arm.

INSTRUCTION

Keep It Tucked!

This downswing right-arm trick keeps your swing on plane and slices at bay

Tuck your right arm against your right side on your downswing—it helps you drop your right shoulder, putting the club on the correct path into impact. If your right arm stays away from your side, your shoulders will turn horizontally, causing an outside-in swing path and weak slices.
—**Dana Rader**

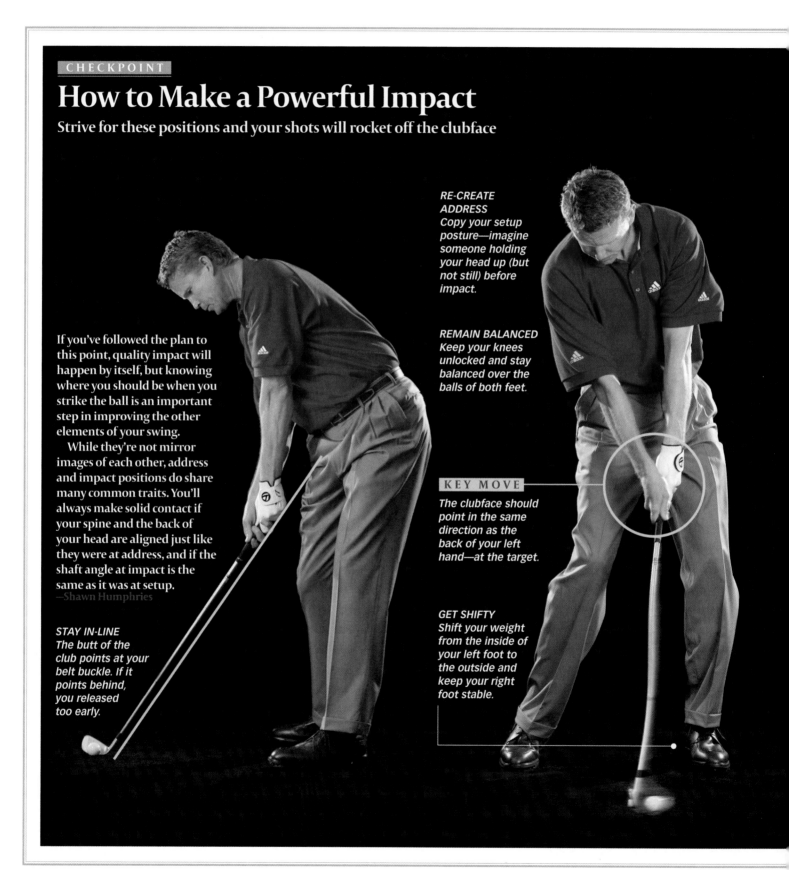

CHECKPOINT

How to Make a Powerful Impact

Strive for these positions and your shots will rocket off the clubface

If you've followed the plan to this point, quality impact will happen by itself, but knowing where you should be when you strike the ball is an important step in improving the other elements of your swing.

While they're not mirror images of each other, address and impact positions do share many common traits. You'll always make solid contact if your spine and the back of your head are aligned just like they were at address, and if the shaft angle at impact is the same as it was at setup.
—Shawn Humphries

STAY IN-LINE
The butt of the club points at your belt buckle. If it points behind, you released too early.

RE-CREATE ADDRESS
Copy your setup posture—imagine someone holding your head up (but not still) before impact.

REMAIN BALANCED
Keep your knees unlocked and stay balanced over the balls of both feet.

KEY MOVE
The clubface should point in the same direction as the back of your left hand—at the target.

GET SHIFTY
Shift your weight from the inside of your left foot to the outside and keep your right foot stable.

Open the Door

Turn your hands like you're opening a door to square up the clubface through impact

1

Retain the hinge in your wrists deep into the downswing. That saves energy for impact.

2

Continue to move your hands while keeping your right shoulder back.

3

Rotate the back of your left hand as if you're turning a doorknob.

4

Open the door so that the back of your left hand faces the target.

5

Keep your arms extended through impact (so you don't chicken wing).

6

Maintain the triangle formed by your arms, hands and shaft.
—Shawn Humphries

How to Avoid Scooped Shots

Keep your right wrist bent for solid strikes

Fault
You try to scoop the ball into the air with your irons and wedges. This instinct to lift leads to mis-hits and missed greens. Here's how to strike your irons pure so you can hit your targets every time.

Fix #1: Slap your hand
Hold your left hand out as shown. Now slap it with your right—see how you make that angle with your right wrist? That angle is the key to a crisp hit. It happens naturally when you slap something because your focus is on the slap, not on getting the ball airborne.

Fix #2: Hit a punch
Take a 7-iron and hit half-swing punch shots with your right arm only. To make solid contact, you'll need a descending blow, which comes from that right-wrist angle mentioned at left. Add your left hand and some weight shift back and through and hit some longer shots. Your ball striking will improve in no time.
—Charlie King

Hit punch shots with one arm to learn how to keep your right wrist bent into impact.

Which Slice Is Your Slice?

Finding the answer is the key to fixing your impact

The predominant ball flight of most recreational players is a slice (a shot that curves wildly from left to right). The first step to stopping your slice is to determine which type of slice is destroying your game. That way you'll know if you have to correct your face angle at impact, your downswing path or both.

POLL
52% of you hit a straight slice

POLL
18% of you hit a pull slice

POLL
30% of you hit a push slice

Straight slice
Your path is solid but your clubface is open at impact. The ball starts straight, then curves.

Pull slice
Your path is outside-in and your clubface is open. The ball starts left, then curves right.

Push slice
Your path is too inside-out and your clubface is open. The ball starts right, then curves farther right.

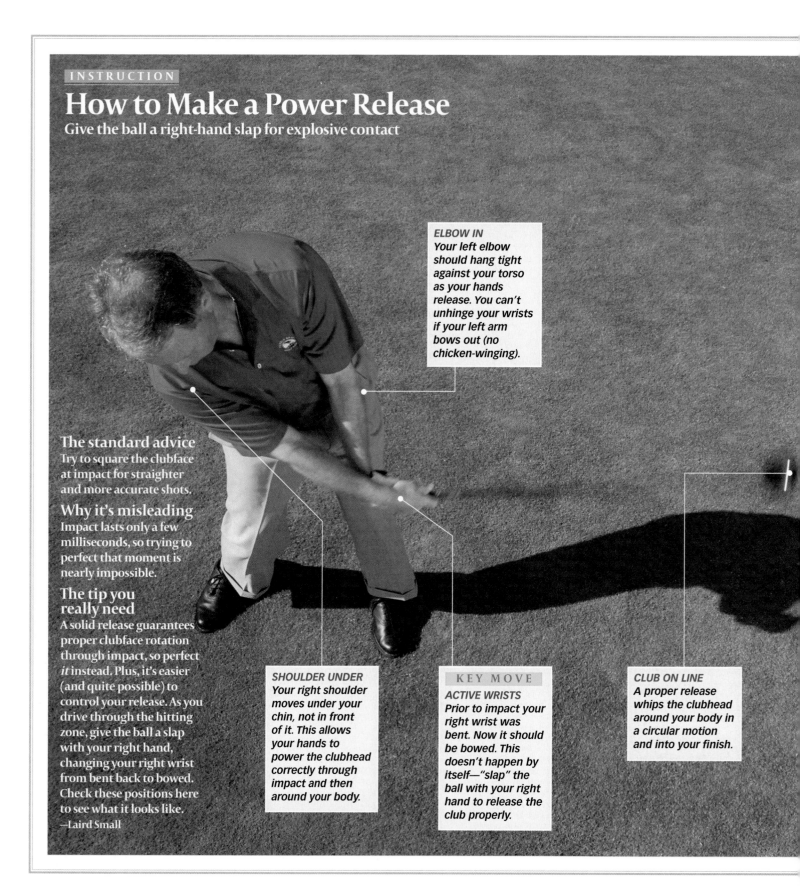

INSTRUCTION

How to Make a Power Release

Give the ball a right-hand slap for explosive contact

ELBOW IN
Your left elbow should hang tight against your torso as your hands release. You can't unhinge your wrists if your left arm bows out (no chicken-winging).

The standard advice
Try to square the clubface at impact for straighter and more accurate shots.

Why it's misleading
Impact lasts only a few milliseconds, so trying to perfect that moment is nearly impossible.

The tip you really need
A solid release guarantees proper clubface rotation through impact, so perfect *it* instead. Plus, it's easier (and quite possible) to control your release. As you drive through the hitting zone, give the ball a slap with your right hand, changing your right wrist from bent back to bowed. Check these positions here to see what it looks like.
—Laird Small

SHOULDER UNDER
Your right shoulder moves under your chin, not in front of it. This allows your hands to power the clubhead correctly through impact and then around your body.

KEY MOVE

ACTIVE WRISTS
Prior to impact your right wrist was bent. Now it should be bowed. This doesn't happen by itself—"slap" the ball with your right hand to release the club properly.

CLUB ON LINE
A proper release whips the clubhead around your body in a circular motion and into your finish.

Wristy Business

Try this drill to improve your release

1 Settle into your stance without a club and take a mock grip with your hands. Flex your right wrist back. Your left wrist will bow automatically. This is exactly where you want to be as you approach impact, with your hands leading the clubhead.

2 Create your release by hinging your right wrist into a bowed position at half speed. Notice how your left wrist bends back as a result and how your body turns and opens slightly to the target to support this action.

3 Continue this drill, picking up speed each time. The faster you do it, the more you should feel like you're "slapping" the ball with your right hand, or flexing it forward like you do when you shoot hoops. That's the feel you're after.

Control Every Shot

You can create any ballflight you want by turning your left-hand knuckles either up or down

Knuckles down is good for...

All full swings, rough escapes and fairway-bunker shots

Knuckle down for power

For maximum speed and distance, gradually rotate your forearms (right over left) and turn your wrists through the hitting zone so that your left-hand knuckles and left elbow point toward the ground in your release.

Why it works

Maximum clubhead acceleration occurs when your hands give in to the force of your downswing and turn over to release your clubhead toe over heel. You know you've reached your power threshold when your left-hand knuckles and left elbow point down in your release.

How to do it

Through the hitting zone, sling the club smoothly past your left thigh by trying to "flick" an imaginary object off your left thumb. Or, think of how you'd turn your left hand out to hitch a ride.

When you need full power and speed, point your left-hand knuckles at the ground.

Knuckles up is good for...

Greenside bunker shots, chips and pitches, knock-downs, bump-and-runs and punch shots.

Knuckle up for control

For shots that require control over raw distance, keep your hands ahead of the clubhead at impact and the back of your left hand pointed toward the sky in your follow-through.

Why it works

You're basically holding off your release, which is the fastest part of your swing. While you'll lose distance (which you don't need on these shots), you'll gain extra accuracy because you're squaring your clubface with your body turn instead of your hands, and big muscles are easier to control than little ones.

How to do it

Through impact, cup your left wrist slightly and lift the back of your left hand toward the sky. This usually produces a scoopy impact, but if you set up with your hands ahead of the ball, your contact will be crisp.

Hit ultra-accurate short-game shots by pointing your left-hand knuckles toward the sky.

DRILL

How to End Your Swing

If you can groove a solid finishing position first, it'll be easier to make the swing moves necessary to finish in balance and eliminate poor ball flight

1 Put on a baseball cap and take your normal address position with an iron.

2 Without moving your feet, stand straight up and bring your club straight up over the top of your head.

3 Make a quarter turn to the left with your face, chest and hips pointing at the target and the butt end of the club pointing to your left. You'll know you're in the ideal finishing position when you feel the shaft lay across the hair on the back of your head where it pokes out from the cap.
—John Elliott

Use Your Finish to Shape Shots

Pre-set your club to hit draws and fades on command

How to hit a draw

Get into your address position and swing to waist-high in your follow-through. Move your arms and club so that...

● Your club points 10 yards right of the target.

● Your right arm is fully extended and in line with your clubshaft.

● The toe of your club points up.

● Get a feel for this position and swing back to the top of your backswing. Notice how your club automatically moves to the inside and around you *[inset below]*. This is the perfect position from which to attack the ball from the inside out.

● When you proceed to play the shot, swing your club in an effort to re-create the feel of the backswing and release that you just rehearsed.

Start here to hit a draw.

Fade top position

How to hit a fade

Swing to a waist-high follow-through from address and move your arms and club so that...

● Your left arm is fully extended and creates an "L" with the clubshaft.

● The toe of your club points right.

● The shaft points 10 feet left of your target.

● Ingrain this feel and then swing back to the top of your backswing. This time, your pre-set fade release automatically makes you take the club more up and to the outside *[inset below],* which is the perfect position to produce left-to-right spin at impact.

● When you proceed to play the shot, swing your club in an effort to re-create the feel of the backswing and release that you just rehearsed.

—**Mike Adams**

Start here to hit a fade.

Draw top position

Here's Proof That Your Finish is Key

A recent student didn't speak English and had never touched a club. I tried to use pictures and video to explain the swing, but that failed. So I took a radical approach.

Step One was to physically place her into a sound address position. Only when she had ingrained this position into her muscle memory was she allowed to make a backswing

Step Two was to physically take her up to the top of the backswing and pause her there.

Step Three was to hit the ball from her static top position. After each swing, I physically adjusted her into a proper finish position and made her hold it for a few counts. I did this for every swing, during every lesson, an hour a day for six days in a row. By the end of the sixth day she was hitting her 7-iron 130 yards with a nice draw.

Pausing at each position was the key. It allowed her to feel what was correct, especially the end point, to give her the feeling of where she needed to be.

Most golfers never truly know if what they feel in their swings is right or wrong, especially when they're finishing their swings off balance and out of control.

—**Mike Bender**

SWING SMOOTHER

Follow these tips to swing tension-free
and power the ball almost effortlessly

DRILL

How to Swing at Your Speed

**Go from too fast or too slow to just right and watch
your shots soar high, far and straight**

Few swing fundamentals are more overlooked than tempo (the consistency
of the pace at which you swing your club). Tempo is a difficult concept to
grasp—there's more to it than swinging your club faster or slower. You need
to feel it. In the same way that you developed your natural walking pace,
you must find your natural swing speed or your motion will lack the
smooth, rhythmic feel associated with solid ball striking.

1
Tee up four balls in a row. Address the one closest to you and hit it at 25 percent of your standard swing speed. Immediately move to the next ball. This time, make a swing at 50 percent speed. Hit the third ball at 75 percent speed and the last at full throttle.

2
Perform this drill a few times. Focus on the feel of the different speeds, and keep in mind that your goal is to become familiar with different tempos, not hit the ball longer or straighter.

3
Swinging at different tempos helps you coordinate the movement of your body and your club to produce solid contact in an effortless fashion. It's this level of control that enables you to follow one long and straight shot with another.
—Pia Nilsson

QUICK TIP
Your downswing should mirror your backswing, and since your arms take the club back, they should swing it down to the ball, too.
—Dan Pasquariello

Get Smooth With the Right Hinge

Time your wrist cock with your body pivot

The problem

You often lose the timing of your swing because you either delay or quicken your wrist hinge in your takeaway. These errors destroy the natural momentum of your club going back, and can do the same on the way back down via a late release or one that occurs far too early in the downswing.

The Solution

Hinge your wrists at the correct time, which varies depending on the iron you have in your hands and the shot you need to play. Adjust the timing of your hinge to create perfect rhythm and tempo.

For full swings with your mid-and long irons...
Simply maintain the hinge that you established at address during your takeaway. Full swings require a longer body pivot, so hinge less and turn more as you bring your hands to waist height. You know you've done it right if your chest points away from the target and the butt of the club is outside your right leg when the shaft is parallel to the ground.

A late hinge creates a late release and poor tempo.

Error on the quick side

You've been told to keep the clubhead low in your takeaway, which is good advice unless you overdo it and remove the hinge in your wrists that was established at address [photo above]. Now you're late on your hinge going back, which means you'll be early on your hinge going forward, and you'll hit the shot fat. As a general rule, hinge your wrists sooner and you'll hear the sweet sound of crisp contact more frequently.

For half-swing shots inside 50 yards, your right wrist should hinge before your hands pass your right knee.

For half-swing shots...
Make a full hinge before your hands pass your right knee. Short swings from 30-60 yards require much less body pivot, which means your wrists must hinge sooner in your backswing. You've done it right if your chest points at your right foot and the butt of the club is on top of your right leg when the shaft is parallel to the ground.
—Dom DiJulia

Be Loose, Not Lazy

Use "downtime" on the course to your tempo's advantage

Fault: You make casual, right-hand-only swings while waiting on the tee box or in the fairway for the group ahead to clear away. While most of these mini-swings are made with the sole purpose of passing time, they'll  ingrain bad habits since you're likely just flipping your club back and through— a big no-no.

Fix: Continue to make your mini-swings when the course backs up, but do so with a purpose. Repeat a solid back-and-forth motion with an eye toward removing tension in your arms and hands. Take it a step further and make sure you're rotating your right hand as the club sweeps beneath you. Turn into your follow-through with the toe of your club pointing up. When it comes time to play your shot, you'll be loose and ready to deliver a smooth, powerful strike.
—John Elliott, Jr.

Make every swing—even the casual ones while waiting for your turn to hit—count.

HIT STRAIGHTER

Try these teacher tricks to find the fairway
or the green with laser-like accuracy

INSTRUCTION

One Minute to Straighter Shots

Watch your watch to create perfect impact every time

In order to control the direction of your shots, you must control the position of the clubface at impact. Unfortunately, knowing exactly where the clubface is pointing throughout your swing is difficult, but you can do it if you focus on something you can see, such as your wristwatch.

Unless your grip is way too strong or very weak, the face of your watch points in the same direction as the clubface. So your goal is to get into the habit of pointing your watch at the target at impact. The position of your watch at impact also can help you discover errors in your swing and clubface position. During your next practice session, watch your watch and you'll find out how to hit straighter shots.

—John Dahl

Where your watch points, the ball will follow.

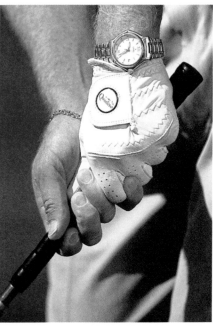

Solid
Straight shots result from squared impact, evidenced by your hands leading the clubface into impact and your watch facing the target.

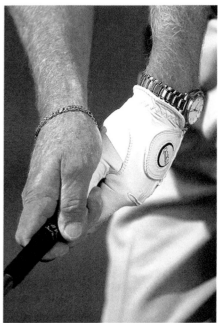

Hook
If your watch points behind you, your swing is guilty of too much arm and hand rotation. The clubface is closed at impact, and the ball is heading left.

Slice
If your watch points to the right of the target (or even remotely skyward), the clubface is open, and you're looking at a banana ball.

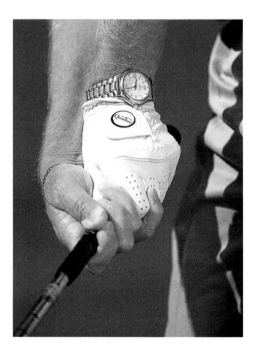

Cast
Great ball strikers have a flat left wrist at impact. If your knuckles get in front of your watch, that's an early release, and you won't know where the ball is going.

INSTRUCTION

How to Tame Your First-Tee Jitters
Mental tips for getting your round off to a solid start

If you get nervous standing over your first tee shot, relax. Even Tour players feel opening-tee jitters at major tournaments and other big events. The best way to beat first-tee pressure is to use your warm-up time to get into a playing mode rather than just bashing balls with no goals in mind. Here are three keys to becoming a cool customer on the first tee.

1 Make sure your pre-round warm-up is exactly that, and not practice. Don't work on swing keys or ask for tips when you have 30 minutes or less until your tee time. Any confusion about technique will only heighten the pressure you feel later.

2 Vary your clubs and distances often, never hitting more than three shots in a row with the same club. Take a cue from well-coached basketball teams. The players don't take countless free throws before a game, but instead hit shots from various spots around the court.

3 Spend the last 10 minutes of your warm-up "playing" the first three holes of the course you're about to tackle. Hit the club you plan to hit off the first tee and then hit the appropriate club for your approach. Go through your pre-shot routine and try to execute the shots exactly as you would on the course. Repeat this for the next two holes. This drill heightens your visualization and helps you narrow your targets. You'll arrive at the first tee ready to play, which will lessen the pressure.
—Richard Coop, Ph.D., GOLF's mental-game consultant

CHECKPOINT

Be a Palm Pilot
Your right hand controls the clubface

A square clubface at impact doesn't guarantee success, but it gives you a much better chance for it.

If you've taken a proper grip, your right palm should mimic the angle of your clubface. So instead of trying to control your clubhead, control your right hand. Make sure your right palm points down at the ball once it reaches your right thigh in your downswing. This forces you to properly hit down on the ball and is a good start to squaring the clubface.
—David Glenz

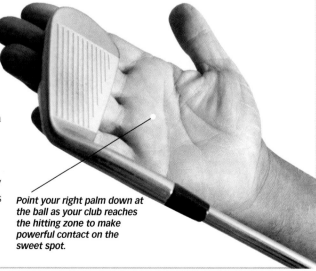

Point your right palm down at the ball as your club reaches the hitting zone to make powerful contact on the sweet spot.

HIT PURER SHOTS

You know when you've crushed it—here's
how to get that feeling time and again

To hit irons solidly
you need to hit
down and compress
the ball between
the ground and
the clubface.

Learn From Your Divots

It's the first step to
ball-first contact

Good iron players hit the ball
first, then the turf. Next time
you're at the range, press a
tee into the ground about
one inch from the ball
outside your target line *[top
photo]*. Hit the ball with your
7-iron. **If you make ball-
first contact, the divot
will be on the target
side of the tee** *[bottom
photo]*. If the divot starts
slightly behind the tee, you
hit it a little fat and sacrificed
distance. If the entire divot is
behind the tee, you chunked
it. Try to hit 10 shots in a row
with your divot starting on
the target side of the tee.

Place a tee opposite your ball
to test your divot pattern.

Your divots should be in front of
the tee and point to the target.

Do You Extend or Flip?

Only one is good for your game

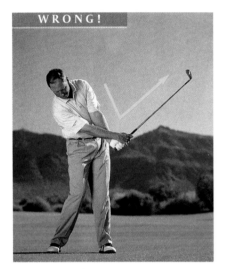

WRONG!

RIGHT!

Flip is not hip

If you hit low-flying skulls, chances are your clubhead is whipping ahead of your hands as you try to scoop the ball into the air *[above]*. That puts the leading edge of the club into contact with the ball. You'll know you're doing it if your clubhead is higher than your hands in your release.

Hit down and through

Hit a series of balls and stop the clubhead below the level of your waist *[above]*. You'll find it impossible to scoop at the ball—and necessary to hit down on it—to achieve this shortened finish. Don't be afraid to shorten your follow-through if you mis-hit a few irons in the middle of your round.

Drop Your Foot Back

It helps you get your weight on your front foot

Address a ball in the middle of your stance while holding a 5-iron. Bend your right knee, point your toe into the ground and hit the ball. By dropping your right foot back, away from the target line, you can't lean away from the target—a classic reverse pivot—as you make your downswing. Instead, you will rotate around your left foot and make a descending blow on the back of the ball.

—Mike Malaska

Hit balls with your right foot back to stop a reverse pivot.

Slot the Club for Solid Drives

Keeping your right arm tucked against your side is the key

Fault: You prematurely release (or cast) the clubhead.

Fix: Take your driver to the top of your swing with your right arm. Hold a plastic bottle against the right side of your torso as shown, then bring your club down to impact. If you squash the bottle before you unhinge your wrists, you delay your release until the moment when it creates the perfect blend of power and accuracy. If you don't, you allowed the clubhead to outrace your hands to the ball, which costs you in yards and missed fairways.

—Robert Baker

1

2

Try to squash a bottle against your right side on your downswing to squeeze out a few extra yards.

CHECK YOUR TECHNIQUE

You know what to do, but are you doing it right? Here's how to find out.

Mirror the Perfect Swing

Use your reflection—and hip turn—to stay on plane from start to finish

Your goal
To create the perfect swing plane. The perfect plane is described as a circle tilted to match the angle of your clubshaft at address. That's a good visual, but you can't attach a hula-hoop to your 7-iron. All you need to perfect your swing plane is masking tape and a mirror.

How to achieve it
Let's assume that your address position is solid, with your back straight, knees flexed and ready for action, and your arms hanging beneath your shoulders. Find a full-length mirror and take your address in front of it. Study your reflection and note the angle of your clubshaft. Place tape on the mirror along this line (we'll call this *Line 1*), and then another in the opposite direction (*Line 2*), so that the two lines intersect at 90 degrees. These lines hold the key to grooving an on-plane swing because they help you get your body and club in the correct positions on both the backswing and the follow-through.
—Mike LaBauve

CHECKPOINT

1. The Address check
At setup, make sure your shaft mimics *Line 1*. Your forward bend toward the ball should position your back and head along *Line 2*. Now you're solid.

Line 1   Line 2

2. The Backswing check

Take your club back to just above waist high and stop. Look at the mirror and make sure your back and head still lie on *Line 2* and that your shoulder turn and wrist hinge have placed the clubshaft along *Line 1*.

If you're not on the correct backswing plane, it's because you lifted the club with your hands more than you turned your upper body (shaft above *Line 1*). Or you whipped the club too far to the inside by turning your shoulders too level and not raising the club at all (shaft below *Line 1*). To get your club correctly on plane, all you need to do is turn your left shoulder under your chin and gently cock your wrists a full 90 degrees.

3. The Follow-through check

Swing through impact and stop when your hands reach just above waist height. Study your reflection to make sure that the shaft rests on *Line 1*, and your head and back haven't strayed from *Line 2*.

The common error here is a clubshaft that lies above *Line 1*, because most golfers don't swing enough to the left, or if they do they don't execute enough hip turn. You really need both: an aggressive and full hip rotation, along with hand movement that brings your club across your chest (not away from it). Although most swings finish with the shaft over the left shoulder (above *Line 1*), the shaft goes left after impact before it travels up.

6 Plane Errors to Avoid

Do any of these swings look familiar? If so, it's time to get back on plane.

It's very difficult to hit solid shots once your club gets off plane. Make a point to check your swing plane in a mirror often to avoid grooving bad habits.

Upright
hands way above shoulders

Hitting under
shaft below shoulder plane

Trapped
club too far behind the body

Over the top
club above shoulder plane

Across the line
shaft points right of target

Laid off
club points way left of target

Get the Perfect Finish

Stretch your left hip flexor to maintain proper posture

With your hands on your hips, make a mock swing and hold your finish. Make sure your weight is over your front foot and your belt buckle faces directly at the target.

Bend your upper body to the right until it matches the angle of Line 2 *[see left]*. Ouch! But it's a great way to stretch your hips and will help you maintain your posture through impact.

Don't expect more distance from swinging harder. Big drives result from widening your swing arc and saving energy for impact. Do both and your swing speed will increase almost automatically.

SECTION 3

YOU AND YOUR DRIVER

How to turn a love-hate relationship into a beautiful friendship—and massive yards

T he key to the modern game is to hit the ball as far as you can and then go find it. Technology provides you the tools to knock it out there, but do you know how to use them? Your driver can't swing itself, nor can you simply move your arms or hips faster to create yardage that isn't there. There are hard, fast rules you must follow. And since your driver is the longest, largest and potentially most dangerous club in your bag, neglecting them pays off in a triple-whammy of lost yards, lost balls and lost strokes.

Once you harness the power of your driver, however, you'll find that playing by the big dog's rules makes the game a whole lot easier. Approach shots become shorter, par 5s become reachable and your confidence soars when you know you can bust one out there anytime you like.

There are three main things you must do to improve your driving distance: Increase the width of your swing, sequence your downswing to add club speed, and learn how to make consistent contact in the center of the clubface. This section touches on all three, with tips to not only make you the big hitter in your regular foursome, but the most accurate one, too.

---

5 THINGS YOU'LL LEARN IN THIS SECTION

- **How to widen your swing arc—the primary ingredient for power-packed drives**
- **How to swing faster without swinging out of your shoes and hitting into trouble**
- **How to hit more fairways—even the narrow ones**
- **Three ways to tame your first-tee jitters and get your round off to a good start**
- **Power drills that give you extra speed at the exact point where you need it most**

YOUR GAME

What Are Your Weak Spots?

Here's what *GOLF Magazine* readers had to say about their driving game in a recent survey.

What's your most common driving mistake?

Not enough distance: 37%

Hooking: 21% Slicing: 33%

What club do you replace most often?

Driver: 42% Putter: 21%

Something else: 26% Fairway woods: 11%

WIDEN YOUR ARC

Big swings begin with a big arc, and the wider the path your clubhead traces from start to finish, the more speed and power you can create to launch the ball deep down the fairway

Picture a light on your back and shine it toward the target.

Turn Your Back to the Target

Light your way to a stronger turn

Fault: You don't turn enough on your backswing when hitting driver.

Fix: Pretend that a light affixed to your right shoulder blade points behind you at address. Swing your driver to the top, turning your right shoulder behind your head until the light shines toward the target. You'll make a complete turn behind the ball, storing energy to be unleashed at impact.
—**Michael Breed**

Three Drills to Get Wider

1. Reach for it

Place your driver on the ground, straight back from your right foot, and put a chair at the other end. Pick up the club and swing it back slowly, trying to nip the chair as you pass it. If the clubhead clears the chair, you're not getting enough extension. If you move the chair on the way back, you're overreaching. A perfect extension just grazes it. Once you've extended to the chair, check that your weight is on your right side.
—**Fred Griffin**

Pass the bucket to build a better swing arc.

2. Do the sit and spin

Hold a bucket of range balls (or fried chicken or anything of similar weight) while sitting forward in a chair. Now turn to your right, as if you were handing the bucket to someone seated beside you. Notice how your head, shoulders and torso all turn together. That's what a full turn feels like, with your body rotated away from the target and your weight balanced over your right side.
—**Craig Shankland**

Extend the club back so it grazes the chair.

Spread Your Wings

Go from narrow to wide by flexing your back

Look at any great driver of the ball and you'll see that the space between his shoulders is the same at impact as it is at address. You'll never see hunched shoulders or bent arms through the hitting area. **Maintaining the distance between your shoulders creates the necessary room for you to swing through impact** and, more importantly, helps you maintain the width of your swing arc for enhanced clubhead speed.

To establish and better retain width, use your back muscles. At setup, bring both hands to ear height with your palms facing outward. As you do, sense how the large muscles of your back bring your shoulder blades closer together and pull your shoulders farther apart. Now, bend from your hips into your normal address posture, keeping your back engaged and your blades pinched together. Now you're set for power.
—Mike Malaska

Pinch your shoulder blades together to get wide at address.

Keep your shoulders apart as you settle into your driving stance.

Re-create wide—not shrugged—shoulders at impact.

3. Add some hip power

To understand the role your hips play as you coil behind the ball on your backswing, try this drill made popular by Julius Boros. If you have a stocky build like Julius (or me!), this drill will help you hit the ball a ton.

Step 1

Set up in your regular driving stance, and then swing your driver back to hip height using only your right arm. Try to extend your right arm as far as you can.

Step 2

Now try to reach over and put your left hand on the grip. Your body gets in the way, right? In order for your left hand to reach the club, you have to rotate your right hip back, which gives you enough room to reach the club. Copy this position on your real swing to build more power.
—Bill Madonna

QUICK TIP
For a stronger coil, try kicking in your right knee at address. This makes your right leg a post so you can turn against resistance.

DRILL

Hand Yourself Extra Yards

This drill will widen your arc and pump up your drives

If you're a short hitter—or simply want to be a longer one—one thing to check is the butt of the club, which should remain as far away from your body as possible, especially at the top. The way to do this is to create as much leverage between your arms as possible—that is, a feeling of the right arm pushing the left one out.

Step 1

Take your normal address position.

Step 2

Lift the fingers of your right hand off the grip, so that only the palm of your right hand touches the club.

Step 3

Start your takeaway by pushing the handle of the club away and behind you using your left hand. As your reach the top of your backswing, push the butt of the club up with your right palm. Continue to push the butt of the club up so that your left arm is perfectly straight.
—Todd Sones

CHECKPOINT

Once you're comfortable with this wider and freer takeaway, grip the club as you normally do and try to re-create that same feeling of leverage and width as you take the club to the top. Note in the sequence below how this leverage and width is maintained at every point: takeaway, top, downswing, impact and follow-through. That's what you should strive for.
—**Todd Sones**

"Create as much leverage between your arms as possible—that is, a feeling of the right arm pushing the left one out."

The lie of your club sets the path.

Leverage begins in the backswing.

Hands as far away from the body as possible.

Club re-traces wide backswing arc.

Arms pulled from the shoulder sockets.

Width maintained in the release.

Width is still evident at the end.

INSTRUCTION

Stretch to 10:30

Move the butt of your club far away from your body

The more distance there is between the butt of your club and the ball when you reach the top, the more room your clubhead has to accelerate on the downswing. When the grip is at 10:30, it's the farthest it should be from the ball. To get it there, swing back while keeping the triangle formed by your shoulders and arms intact. If your grip hits 12:00, your arms probably have folded, collapsing the triangle and reducing your power.—**Martin Hall**

CHECKPOINT

How to Get Wide From the Start

Pre-set your hips for an upswing

Set up to a ball with a driver, then pick up the club and hold it across your hips. You want the club to point up slightly (about a 10-degree angle) from your right hip to your left hip. If your club is parallel to the ground or sloping down, your swing path will be too steep and you'll lose yards. If it's pointing up as shown, you'll set up your swing to trace a wider arc, approach the ball from the inside and sling the club through impact with explosive results.
—**Rick Martino**

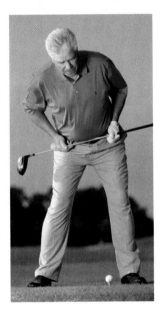

DRILL

Take a Hike!
Another way to add leverage

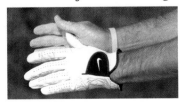

Without a club, set your hands like a quarterback ready to receive the snap from center, with the lifeline of your right hand placed firmly on top of your left thumb. Make a mock backswing and try to maintain the pressure from your right hand on your left thumb all the way to the top. You know you've done it right if you feel your right hand push your left arm out.
—**Tim Mahoney**

HOW TO ADD SPEED

Even just a few miles per hour of extra clubhead speed can be the difference between hitting a mid-iron and a long iron on your approach

INSTRUCTION

Nail Drives With the O-Factor

What is the O-Factor?
The angle of your hips in relation to horizontal.

How to use it
Turn your left hip up and to the left of the target immediately at the start of your downswing—and keep turning it!

What it does
The move is so powerful that it literally pulls your shoulders and arms along for the ride. And since your hips move first, everything else must accelerate to catch up at impact. Using your hips like this is what allows you to hammer the ball without swinging hard.
—Robert Baker

Address
Set your body like an airplane coming in for a landing, with your left shoulder and left hip above their right-side counterparts, and your spine tilted away from the target.

Backswing
Turn against the resistance of your right thigh, not your entire lower body, and make sure you rotate your shoulders and your hips. This allows you to create maximum energy.

O-Positive
At address, your O-Factor should be slightly positive. As you settle into your stance, bump your left hip up to set your body at the correct angle.

O-Neutral
You're balanced and loaded up with power if your hip angle shifts back to zero while your spine remains tilted away from the target.

Downswing

From the top, turn your hips immediately to the left and, as the club approaches impact, pull your left hip up. This creates whip-like speed and helps drop your club onto the correct plane.

O-Positive

Kick in your right knee to get your left hip moving up and your right shoulder moving down.

How to Groove Your O-Factor

Perform these drills to improve your hip action and gas up your swing

Make a hip swing

To learn the feeling of powering your downswing with your hips, place your driver behind your back as shown, make your backswing turn and, as you rotate through impact, keep your upper body as quiet as possible. Make a level turn going back and use "butt power" to whip your left hip up and around on your downswing.

Whip your hips and let your left arm fold in your follow-through.

Angled shaft matches angled hips.

Level shaft matches level hips.

Left hip up, right shoulder down.

Fling your headcover

With your left hand, swing a headcover over your right shoulder and slap your back, then use your hips to whip it forward. Keep your left arm in and try to smack your back with the headcover on your follow-through.
—Robert Baker

Fingers First

A palm grip only slows you down

Your hands represent one of three power sources in your swing (your arms and your pivot are the other two). To use them correctly, start by gripping the club in your fingers. Think about a major league pitcher: When he wants to bring the heat, he grips the ball in his fingers. When he wants to take something off a pitch, he holds the ball in his palm. When you hold the club in your palms it limits your ability to release the club. A palm grip also creates tension because you have to squeeze tighter to hold the club, and that dramatically decreases clubhead speed. How important is a finger grip? It's the first thing you should consider in the search for more power.
—Sandy LaBauve

A palm grip robs you of speed.

A finger grip adds speed.

INSTRUCTION

Turn Your Swing Into a Sling

Sling apples to release all the power in your swing

To feel the proper acceleration and rhythm of the clubhead in your downswing, use this image made famous by Sam Snead. Imagine there's an apple stuck to the center of the shaft. (Snead used to cut out the core of an apple and slide it over a hickory stick.) As you start down from the top, feel the apple begin sliding down the shaft until it flies off the end just after impact. You should feel like you're slinging the apple at or beyond the ball. This image delays the clubhead at the start of the downswing just enough so that your arms and body can work in sync and transfer full energy to the ball at impact.
—**Martin Hall**

1

Feel the apple slide down during your downswing...

2

...and sling it pass the ball after impact.

"Start your downswing by 'firing' your right side. Kick your right foot and knee toward the target. This shifts your weight to your left side and sets your hip turn in motion.
—**Jimmy Ballard**

Go Wide for Speed

This right-foot trick gives you extra yards

Sometimes you have to carry the ball 10 or 15 yards farther than usual to clear a hazard or to position your drive on a reachable par 5. To get that boost, try this: Widen your stance by sliding your right foot about a foot's width away from the target. This will set your upper body well behind the ball, promoting an ascending strike. It will also give you more time to release the clubhead and crush the ball.

—**Michael Breed**

Widening your right foot gives your swing more time to accelerate.

Pull Down for Power

This drill helps you release with max power

Most golfers throw the clubhead at the ball, which reduces leverage too soon. You want to keep the clubhead away from the ball for as long as possible on your downswing. To help you accomplish this, try gripping a club as you normally would, but with about two inches of separation between your hands. **Take a few swings with this split grip, pulling down with your left hand on the downswing while pulling back with the fingers of your right hand.** This creates the latest release possible—you can't release the club early—and tremendous speed.

—**Phil Ritson**

How to Stripe Your Opening Tee Shot

Ask yourself these three questions to find the right fix for you

Don't aim at a target 300 yards away; pick one three inches away instead.

Q: Do you get more nervous over the first tee shot of the day or a pressure putt late in the round?

53%—First tee shot
24%—Pressure putt
15%—Don't get nervous

1
IS IT FIRST-TEE JITTERS?
It's common to feel nerves on the first tee, which can make you guide your shot, instead of making an aggressive swing.

2
AM I TRYING TO MAKE A PERFECT SWING?
The fairway looks extra small on the first tee before you're into the round. You may try to make a perfect swing, which causes tension.

3
AM I PULLING THE WRONG CLUB?
Golfers often hit driver with trouble left and right, when a nice little fairway wood would do.

You know if...
You kill it on the range, but you feel like the whole world is watching when you stand on the first tee.

You know if...
Check your recent scorecards. If you struggle on the first couple of holes, you're making the shots harder than they are.

You know if...
Your instinct is to go with a safer club like a 5-wood, but you pull driver to keep up with your buddies. You're giving in to peer pressure.

How to fix it
Make pre-round range bets with your pals—wager, say, a beer, that you can hit a distant green, or nail the ball picker-upper. That gets you used to playing with pressure so the first tee shot is a piece of cake.

How to fix it
Be like Jack. Nicklaus liked to pick a target three inches in front of his ball—a blade of grass, a leaf—and aim at that *[illustration, left]*. Don't even bother looking down the fairway once you're set.

How to fix it
Obey your inner caddie, not your inner Daly. Hit the club that gives you the best chance of finding the fairway. Better 220 from the fairway than 180 from the trees.

—**Rick Grayson**

HIT IT LONGER

A wider swing arc and greater clubhead speed help the yards add up. Here's what you need to put the two together to make you consistently—and scary—long.

DRILL

How to Make a Power Pivot

It's all about staying on plane

How can you hit it flush time after time? The simplest way is to rotate your shoulders on a consistent plane from setup through impact. That means no rising or dipping. Try this drill.

Tee a ball and take your address. Then cross your arms and hold a club against your chest with the grip end at your left shoulder. Turn as if you were swinging to the top and point the grip at the ball. Then mimic your downswing and point the clubhead at the ball.

This power drill will train you to turn your shoulders on a single plane for consistent contact—the first step toward booming tee shots.
—Jim Murphy

Turn your shoulders on a single plane for consistent power off the tee.

Hit the Hot Spot

Make contact high on the face and spot yourself 10 extra yards

You've almost certainly heard Tour players and TV commentators talking about how the sweet spot on drivers has moved from the center to nearer the top of the clubface. The name for this 21st-century sweet spot is the hot spot.

The discovery of the hot spot signals a new era in the evolution of the golf swing. It has happened before: Hickory shafts changed to steel, blade irons changed to cavity back, and wood clubheads changed to metal—all these changes produced shifts in how players strike the ball. In short, the way the game is played largely depends on the equipment of the day. The huge-headed drivers are here to stay, so here's how to reap their benefits and start hitting your longest drives ever.

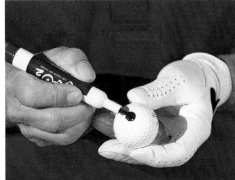

1 *Mark your ball with a dot the size of a shirt button, and place it on the tee so you'll make contact with it.*

2 *Note where your longest shots make a mark and tee the equator of your ball to that spot every time.*

Find Your Hot Spot

Why are the world's best players hitting the ball longer than ever before? Their secret is clear—in some cases, contact is being made on the top scoring line of the clubface! This produces the high-launch, low-spin ballflight that translates into extra yards.

No matter which brand of driver you hit, the hot spot is above the center of the clubface. But it's slightly different for each driver. To find yours, take an erasable marker and put a circle on your ball *[top photo]*. Tee it up with the circle pointing straight back at your clubface at address.

Now hit some drives. After each one examine the clubface to see the circular mark *[bottom photo]*. When you catch one flush, the mark will be high. That's your new sweet spot.

Align the equator of the ball with your hot spot every time and you'll hit long drives more consistently.

—**Peter Kostis**

Try a Power Shift

Drive your weight toward the target

Want distance? Make sure you're shifting your weight toward the target on the downswing. To check your weight shift, take your address with a driver, then tee a second ball just inside your back ankle *[inset photo, right]*. Make your normal swing, moving your weight away from the target going back and toward it coming down. If you transfer your weight correctly, your back ankle will roll inward on the downswing, knocking the second ball off the tee. If you don't bump the ball, you're leaving yards on the table.

—**Ted Sheftic**

Your ankle should knock the ball off the tee with the correct forward weight shift.

HIT EVERY FAIRWAY

Long drives are good.
Long and straight drives
are even better.

DRILL

Extend for Accuracy

This drill will eliminate your cut shot

Fault: You miss too many fairways.

Fix: Tee up a ball and place a second tee six inches and 45 degrees outside the first tee as shown. Try to sweep the ball off of the first tee and swing over the second tee as you sling your clubhead through the hitting area. Performing this drill correctly simulates the feeling of proper extension through impact, stopping you from cutting across the ball (slice) or swinging too much from the inside (push or hook).
—Brian Mogg

Max acceleration occurs after impact, but only if you achieve full extension through the ball.

What Starts Your Move Back Down?

On the downswing with a driver, should the legs move the hips or should the hips move the legs?

Hips move the legs: 57%

Hips and legs work together: 7%

Legs move the hips: 36%

"Your backswing and forward swing start from the ground up and. As the old song goes, 'the hip bone's connected to the thigh bone.' Take this as your legs move your hips, not the other way around."
—**Rick McCord**

"Your legs are like the legs on a tripod—they hold up the top. Legs react, they do not act."
—**Mike Perpich**

"Your hips should lead. In fact, they should begin to turn forward before you finish your backswing."
—**Jon Tattersall**

Shorten Your Finish for Safer Driving

Try this quick tip to split the fairway every time

The problem
Not only do you spray your drives, but you take the anxiety over your sprayed drives to every tee.

The solution
Instead of swinging into your normal full follow-through, finish your drives when the clubhead reaches about waist high after impact. Call this spot "Checkpoint Charlie," and go through the following list when you reach it:

● *The clubshaft and your left arm are more or less still in line*

● *Your right wrist is still bent back slightly*

● *Your right arm is across the middle of your torso*

● *Your chest is pointing directly at the target*

● *The toe of the clubhead is pointing up, neither too open nor too closed*

If you work on finishing your driver swings with a short follow-through that satisfies the five conditions above, you may lose a little distance, but you'll also land a lot more shots on the short grass.
—**Martin Hall**

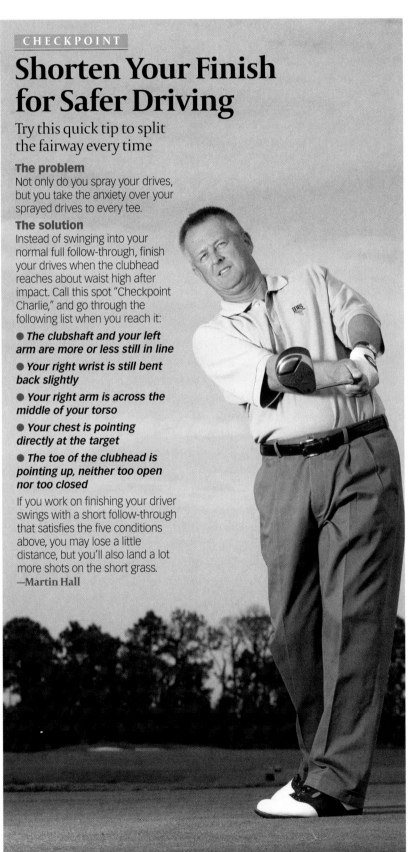

Don't Flex Toward the Ball

Proper knee movement makes flush contact easy

If you kick your back knee toward the ball on your downswing, solid contact becomes nearly impossible. Instead, drive your back knee toward the target as you start down, and begin to post your front knee by straightening it. This creates a wall that everything slings past with maximum force and helps produce flush contact with less sidespin.
—**Paul Trittler**

WRONG!

Don't straighten your right leg as you swing to the top.

RIGHT!

Instead, retain the flex in your right knee.

Don't drive your right knee toward the ball on the way back down.

Instead, drive it toward the target.

Choke Down for Control

When you absolutely must find the fairway, your 3-wood is the best bet. The shorter shaft of a 3-wood gives you greater control. But if you insist on hitting driver, grip down an inch or two on the handle. This effectively shortens the club, making it play more like a fairway wood, but gives you the advantages of the larger clubhead.
—**Michael Breed**

Thanks to technology and our teachers' top tips, you can stretch your scoring zone to 200 yards and beyond.

SECTION 4

HYBRIDS, WOODS & LONG IRONS

They're easier to play than ever. Here's how to use them to make more long-range birdies.

You expect to get the ball close to the flagstick with your short irons and wedges. With longer clubs, however, you're happy with just getting the ball close to the green. It's time to change that line of thinking. Technology has made long irons, fairway woods and hybrids much easier to play, and the swing to get you to birdie range from long distance is the same you'd use with your 8-iron, minus a few adjustments to your setup to create a more sweeping type of impact. The Top 100 Teachers show you the quick way to make that happen on the following pages, so there's no reason you shouldn't expect to hit shots with longer clubs as close to the pin as you do with your more traditional scoring irons.

The challenge is to plan your attack in a way that minimizes the damage when you do miss with your woods and long irons. That means choosing the right landing spot, selecting the right club and using the lay of the land to shape the shot once the ball hits the ground. The Top 100 Teachers have you covered here, too, with strategic ways to get the most out of your long game.

5 THINGS YOU'LL LEARN IN THIS SECTION

- How to hit long irons on the sweet spot consistently
- How to get the most out of your hybrids
- The setup and swing changes necessary to sweep the ball powerfully off the turf with your fairway woods
- How to hit long-iron "stingers" off the tee and from the fairway to control spin and trajectory
- Drills to help you hit your long irons and woods farther and with greater accuracy

Lowdown on Hybrids

What confuses you most about golf equipment?

21% — **Hybrids**
10% — Balls
9% — Wedges
7% — Drivers
7% — Irons
25% — Confused? Not me!

What makes hybrids work
In a word, gravity. The simple physics behind the hybrid's success is its low, deep center of gravity (CG). Because the club's CG is below that of the ball's, the collision of the club and ball at impact produces a higher launch angle and spin rate. A deep CG also directs the clubhead to the ball at a higher effective loft angle, which again increases launch angle and spin rate.

One other element helps the club get the ball up quickly: a flexible shaft bending forward just prior to impact.

The guts of a hybrid reveal the secret to its success: a low, deep center of gravity.

LONG-IRON SECRETS

Use these special swing adjustments to knock down the flagstick with your 3-, 4- and 5-irons

INSTRUCTION

How to Catch Long Irons Flush

Try this tip to make contact on the sweet spot more often

Fault
You hit long irons super thin.

Why you're doing it
You're making a big backswing shift to power up behind the ball *[photo, right]*, but you're getting stuck there on your downswing. This moves the bottom of your swing arc back so you catch the ball on the upswing.

Fix
Get balanced at address and maintain that balance throughout your swing.
—Tim Mahoney

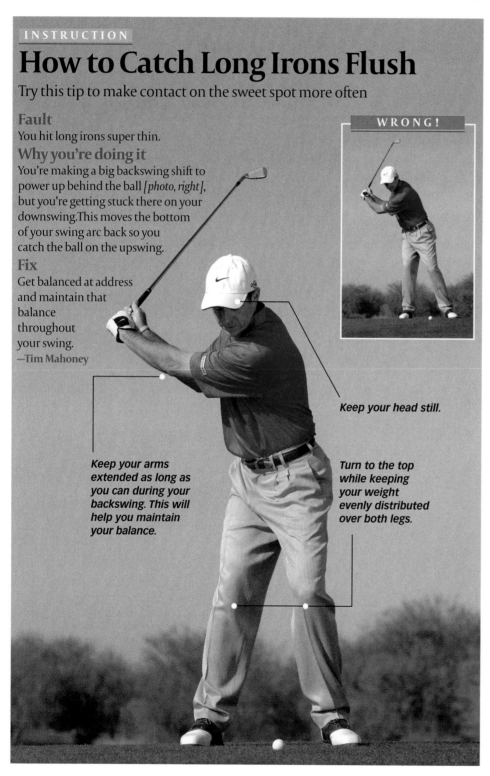

WRONG!

Keep your head still.

Keep your arms extended as long as you can during your backswing. This will help you maintain your balance.

Turn to the top while keeping your weight evenly distributed over both legs.

DRILL

How to Hit Your Long Irons Farther

We studied five iron distance drills—this one works the best

Take your normal address and then pull your feet together. Try to make swings without losing your balance. This drill boosts distance by improving the quality of impact. It also helps you to avoid an out-to-in swing path, since it's hard to swing out-to-in from this position without falling over. While the test results showed a statistically insignificant increase in clubhead speed, an improved path contributed to more center-face hits and a 13-yard average increase in carry distance.
—Eric Alpenfels

Set your feet together to make better contact and add yards.

INSTRUCTION

How to Sting It

Make these three simple changes to hit long irons that fly low, straight and hot

What it is
The "2+2+2", a low-trajectory long iron.

When to use it
Off the tee on tight driving holes and when playing into the wind.

How to hit it
Take your normal address position, then add up the 2s.
—Mike Adams

2

ADD FLARE
Open your stance two inches by flaring out your left foot. This squares your shoulders to your target line, shortens your backswing and gets your weight left— all keys to hitting the ball low.

2

CHOKE DOWN
Choke down about two inches on the grip. This will not only shorten your club and subtract yards from your swing, but it will also stiffen the shaft, which will help produce lower, more boring shots.

2

BALL BACK
Move the ball two inches back in your stance from where you'd normally play it with the chosen club. If you usually play the ball in the center of your stance, move it two inches toward your right foot.

FAIRWAY WOODS

Here's how to hit them sweet to reach par 5s in two and own a go-to option off the tee on short par 4s

Three Musts for Fairway Woods

Follow these rules to sweep the ball powerfully off the turf

1. Position it

Set up with the ball just inside an imaginary line that stretches down from your left armpit. This ball position helps create the sense that you're setting up "behind" the ball at address and allows you to…

Play the ball off your left armpit.

2. Sweep it

One of the biggest mistakes you can make when hitting fairway woods is to feel like you're picking up the club on your backswing and then hitting down on the ball through impact.

Sweep the clubhead back, don't lift it.

To avoid this mistake, sweep the clubhead along the ground to create extension in your backswing, until your natural hip and shoulder turn lifts it off the ground (instead of your arms). As you continue your backswing, concentrate on bringing your left arm over your right shoulder. This motion will help you swing the club around your body, rather than bringing it straight up and down. Once you do that, relax and…

3. Let the loft do its job

The shallow path you established during your backswing puts the club into a position where you don't have to "help" the ball into the air— the loft on the clubface will do that for you. Once the ball is airborne, continue to sweep the club along the ground until your body lifts the clubhead into your follow-through.

—Todd Anderson

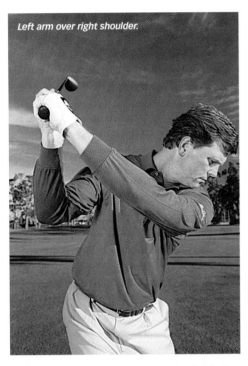

Left arm over right shoulder.

Continue to sweep the club after impact.

Start from a high tee and work down to hitting off the turf.

Practice Your Sweep Move

It only takes 30 swings to get the move down right

If you're uncomfortable trying to pick the ball cleanly off the turf with your fairway woods, grab a bucket of 30 range balls and do the following.

● Hit 10 shots with your 3-wood, teeing up each ball so that half of the ball is above the top of the clubhead.

● Lower the tee to just above ground level and hit 10 more balls.

● Finally, hit 10 3-wood shots off the turf.

By gradually lowering the ball height, you'll learn that the sweeping swing that works when the ball is teed up can do the trick when it's on the ground.

—Bryan Gathright

Roll It Away

Here's another way to make your fairway woods a sweeping success

You've already learned that the wider your swing, the more clubhead speed you can generate. This applies to your fairway woods as well as your driver and irons. Practice making a wider arc by placing a ball behind your 3-wood at address, then initiate your swing by rolling the ball straight back. Starting low and slow will help you establish more width and crank up your fairway woods.

—Carol Preisinger

INSTRUCTION

How to Crush Your Woods

This tip turns your clubs into cannons

Fault

You're not hitting your fairway woods as long as you'd like.

Why it's happening

You're shortening your swing radius in the hope that a more compact swing will help you sweep the ball cleanly off the fairway turf.

Fix

Keep your left arm straight during your backswing. Try increasing your right-hand grip pressure. If you maintain pressure from your right hand on your left thumb, your left arm will remain straight. This creates a wider arc and allows you to extend fully and catch the ball powerfully at impact.

—Tim Mahoney

WRONG!

A loose grip makes for short arms and thin contact.

RIGHT!

Keep your hands connected for a wide arc and flush contact.

HOW TO HIT YOUR HYBRIDS

They're the most versatile clubs in your bag, but only if you use the right technique

INSTRUCTION

Hybrid Off the Tee

Think ankles and hips to generate power and control

Why it works

A hybrid is shorter than a driver, which makes it inherently easier to control. It also features more loft, and more loft creates more backspin and less sidespin (the spin that sends your ball off to the left or right). A long iron used to be a good driving alternative, but a hybrid beats even that. Its face has the same bulge and roll features of a driver that add corrective spin and draw or fade your ball back into the fairway.

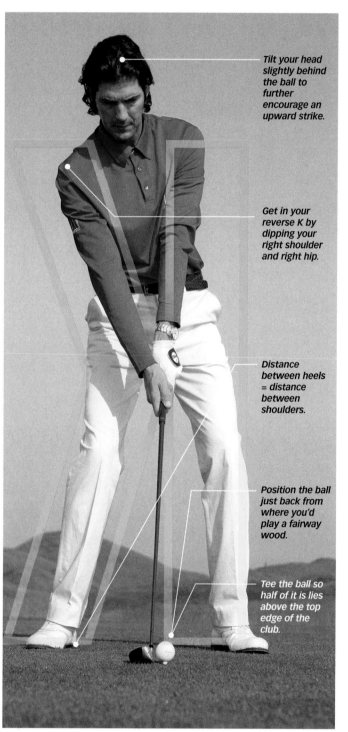

Tilt your head slightly behind the ball to further encourage an upward strike.

Get in your reverse K by dipping your right shoulder and right hip.

Distance between heels = distance between shoulders.

Position the ball just back from where you'd play a fairway wood.

Tee the ball so half of it is lies above the top edge of the club.

Roll and sweep it off the tee

The tilt you establish at address with your "reverse K" [photo, left] must be maintained until impact since it's what allows you to catch the ball on the upswing. Lose your tilt and you'll hit down on the ball—exactly what you don't want.

From the top, roll your ankles toward the target. This simple move has powerful implications. It shifts your weight forward, drops the club into the perfect delivery position, keeps your head behind the ball and, most importantly, saves the energy of your core section for impact. Notice how rolling your ankles whips your knees into action and opens your hips.

After you roll your ankles, drive through the ball by turning your right shoulder and hip toward the target. At the same time, pull your left shoulder toward the sky. This move helps you maintain the tilt you established at address so you can catch the ball on the upswing.
—Robert Baker

Roll your ankles toward the target.

Hybrid From the Fairway

Coil behind the ball like you're hitting a driver

Get your pants pocket behind you

There's a saying that when the ball is down, hit down. Not so fast. A hybrid from the fairway requires the same sweeping motion as the tee shot. Contact with the ground is OK; divots, however, are not.

To make a solid sweep you must rotate your body behind the ball with your right side on your backswing. Use the classic Greg Norman tip: "Get your right pants pocket behind you." As you turn to the right, feel how your left hip and knee are pulled away from the target. That's the sensation of coil—the stored energy that you release into the ball at impact.

During the takeaway, coil your left shoulder, hip and knee against the resistance of your right thigh.

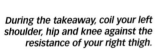

DRILL

How to Kick-Start Your Downswing

Your knees are the key to bring every green into range

Kicking in your right knee on your downswing is an easy move that "breaks" your right leg, making your entire right side shorter and positioning your right shoulder below your left. This sets you up to get your hybrid club under the ball and launch it high toward your target. To practice this move, place your clubhead with the face slightly open just below your right knee and grab the hosel. Now, kick your knee in (while raising your right heel) and close the face. That's the action you want on your downswing when swinging a hybrid.

—Robert Baker

Soaring to New Heights

Results from our exclusive launch-monitor test will convince you that it's time to buy a hybrid

It's no secret that hybrids are easy to rip high and long. But how exactly do they stack up against other clubs of similar loft?

The Test

Four of our testers—handicaps 0, 8, 14 and 25—hit dozens of balls with four Nike Golf clubs: a 3-iron, a 7-wood, an iron-based hybrid and a wood-based hybrid. All had 21 degrees of loft, except for the 3-iron, which was 20 degrees. Hooked up to a launch monitor, the testers hit the clubs in varying order. Only well-struck shots were recorded, and we averaged the testers' totals.
Here's how the clubs fared.

Type of Club	Shaft length (inches)	Clubhead speed (mph)	Ball speed (mph)	Launch angle (degrees)	Apex (feet)	Flight time (seconds)	Backspin (rpm)	Sidespin (rpm)	Carry (yards)
3-iron	39	91	132	7.6	33	4.2	3,269	691	175
Iron-based hybrid	40¾	93	134	8.8	49	5.0	3,889	798	187
7-wood	41½	94	134	9.4	55	5.3	4,219	707	197
Wood-based hybrid	39¾	94	132	9.6	61	5.6	4,647	420	199

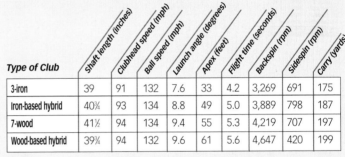

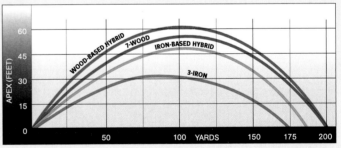

What Hybrid Works Best?

There are wood-based and iron-based hybrids. Wood-based hybrids often have larger faces, for a bigger effective hitting area and added forgiveness, and in general, have a lower and deeper center of gravity than iron-based ones. That means wood-like hybrids get the ball higher and with less effort, to maximize carry distance. By contrast, iron-like hybrids offer you more workability and trajectory control (which is why better players gravitate to these clubs).

A Tour-quality short-iron game begins with selecting the correct part of the green to land your ball on and building a swing that favors accuracy over distance.

SECTION 5

SCORING SHOTS

You should attack the pin with your shortirons. Here's how to do it with max control.

E ven if you hit every fairway you won't do your scores much good if you miss on your approach, especially from scoring range (any distance you can comfortably hit with a 7-iron or less). Here is where you have the easiest chance to knock the ball close. After all, these are short irons with lots of loft that give you more backspin and less sidespin (with fewer hooks and slices as a result). The trick is to build a short-iron swing that favors accuracy, not distance. If you need to hit the ball farther, switch to a longer club.

Swinging a short iron is no different than swinging your driver or fairway woods. But since your short clubs are shorter and sit on a steeper angle at address, you must make a more upright swing. In this section, the Top 100 Teachers share their secrets on how to get the job done right.

While a great short-iron swing doesn't guarantee more birdies, it certainly helps. You also must pick the right part of the green to hit to and learn how to adjust when caught at those tricky distances inside 100 yards. The Top 100 have plenty to say on that, too, so get ready to go low.

5 THINGS YOU'LL LEARN IN THIS SECTION

- How to correctly swing your short irons and wedges
- What to look for on the green to choose the spot that will give you the easiest birdie putt
- How to hit four distances with every wedge in your bag and add spin to make your short approaches bite
- An easy trick to help you make pure contact in the center of the sweet spot and with a square clubface
- When to attack the pin and when to play it safe

Tighten Up Your Weak Links

What area of your game would you like to improve most? Here's what *GOLF Magazine* readers had to say in a recent survey.

Here are your trouble spots

Driving: 19%
Approach shots: 30%
Chipping: 15%
Something else: 21%
Putting: 15%

"Don't be intimidated by the complexity of the golf swing. It's similar to some everyday tasks. Think of chopping wood or swinging a hammer. You hold the implement with your hands and use your arms to apply the power. Same for golf. As you swing, picture one of those activities. You won't think technique; you'll swing the club back with your hands and then forward with your arms as though it were one easy motion."

—Manuel de la Torre

THE SHORT-IRON SWING

From scoring range, use a swing that favors accuracy over distance

Set your hands an inch ahead of the ball with short irons.

On your downswing, shift your weight first then rotate.

3 Musts for Short Irons

Start scoring with your scoring clubs

1. Quit pressing

The loft on your 8- and 9-irons is enough to produce towering approach shots. However, many players press their hands too far forward at address, which delofts the clubface. Instead, try this: Play the ball in the middle of a narrow stance and set your hands about an inch ahead of the ball. Also, flare your front foot slightly to pre-set your turn through the shot.

2. Shift and turn

The best players rotate their hips and shoulders as much with short irons as they do with the driver. Start your downswing by shifting your lower body toward the target, then turn your hips through. You may feel the clubhead lagging—that's OK. By shifting first, then rotating, you'll create room for your hands and arms to sling the club through last.

Swing your clubhead toward the target for extra accuracy.

3. Swivel to the finish

Don't try to steer the club into the ball. Instead, concentrate on swinging the clubhead toward the target. You should also allow your head to swivel forward to encourage momentum down the target line. Your torso and hips should point just left of the target at the finish, and your weight should be over your front foot.

—Kip Puterbaugh

Pick the Right Club

Run through this checklist every time you're at an in-between distance

You're in the fairway and thinking birdie, but the sprinkler head says you're between clubs. Which one should you hit? This chart will give you the answer.
—Jerry Mowlds

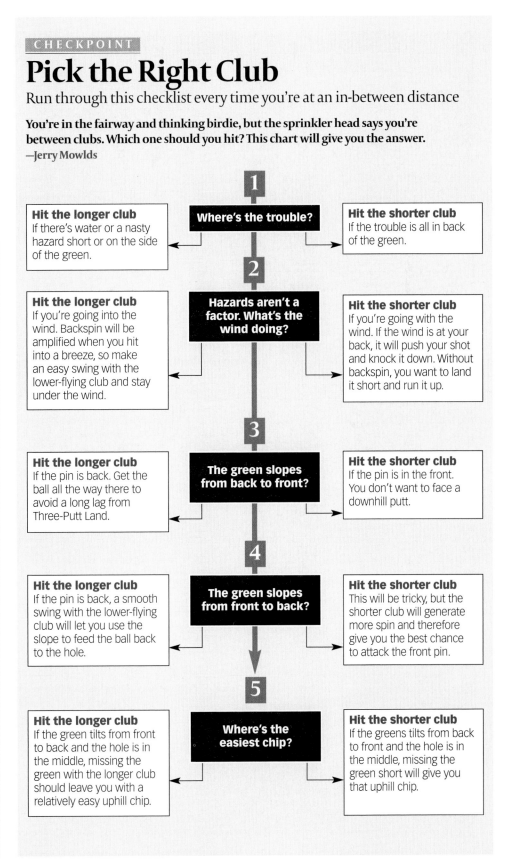

1 — Where's the trouble?

Hit the longer club
If there's water or a nasty hazard short or on the side of the green.

Hit the shorter club
If the trouble is all in back of the green.

2 — Hazards aren't a factor. What's the wind doing?

Hit the longer club
If you're going into the wind. Backspin will be amplified when you hit into a breeze, so make an easy swing with the lower-flying club and stay under the wind.

Hit the shorter club
If you're going with the wind. If the wind is at your back, it will push your shot and knock it down. Without backspin, you want to land it short and run it up.

3 — The green slopes from back to front?

Hit the longer club
If the pin is back. Get the ball all the way there to avoid a long lag from Three-Putt Land.

Hit the shorter club
If the pin is in the front. You don't want to face a downhill putt.

4 — The green slopes from front to back?

Hit the longer club
If the pin is back, a smooth swing with the lower-flying club will let you use the slope to feed the ball back to the hole.

Hit the shorter club
This will be tricky, but the shorter club will generate more spin and therefore give you the best chance to attack the front pin.

5 — Where's the easiest chip?

Hit the longer club
If the green tilts from front to back and the hole is in the middle, missing the green with the longer club should leave you with a relatively easy uphill chip.

Hit the shorter club
If the greens tilts from back to front and the hole is in the middle, missing the green short will give you that uphill chip.

How to Stop Missing the Sweet Spot

Practice cross-handed to groove solid contact

The problem

You thought you had your swing grooved, but a rash of poor shots proves otherwise.

The solution

Using a 7-iron on the practice tee, switch the position of your hands on the grip (left below right) and swing cross-handed. It will feel awkward at first, but if you stick with it you'll ingrain the following swing keys that are difficult to perfect using a normal grip.
—John Elliott, Jr.

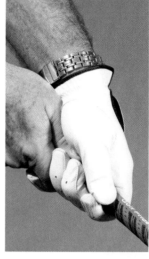

1 Needed hinge

Since your right hand is on top, your right wrist will hinge sooner in your backswing and establish an extra lever for power.

2 Proper arm positioning

The cross-handed grip forces your right arm to follow the lead of your left—it will fold correctly as your left arm remains straight.

3 The power approach

You'll also feel a bent right elbow and an extended left arm deep into your downswing —both are vital to compress the ball and add power.

Set Your Short Clubs Correctly

Hit it purer with a little forward press

There's no way to hit solid iron shots consistently if your hands don't lead the clubhead into the ball. That's the ideal position, and most of you aren't getting there. One reason is a faulty shaft angle at address—hands set behind the clubface—which causes all sorts of mis-hits. If you tilt the shaft toward the target at address, it'll go a long way toward helping you hit it pure.
—**J.D. Turner**

WRONG!   RIGHT!

Address: Hands ahead

Take your grip, then push your hands toward the target so the butt of the club points just in front of your belt buckle *[above right]*. Make sure to keep the clubface square to the target line as you do this, rather than turn the face open. Placing your hands ahead should feel more powerful; it puts the club in a "trapping" position. This is probably a new sensation, as most golfers are used to setting the shaft back *[above left]* and swinging up on the ball to help get it airborne.

Backswing: Pre-set your hinge

Setting up with the shaft leaning forward has another benefit: It pre-sets your backswing wrist hinge. In fact, your right wrist is already slightly hinged by virtue of the shaft leaning forward. Starting from this position gives your backswing a head start and guarantees a full and power-rich hinge. By contrast, when the shaft leans back at address, the clubhead has a lot of catching up to do. With the wrists hinged at the top, you have the best chance of a solid, hands-ahead strike at the bottom.

Punch Your Way to Lower Scores

This low power play checks up quick

Why you need it
The punch flies with a piercing, lower-than-normal trajectory that, amazingly, stops with more spin than a shot hit with your standard full swing.

When to play it
The classic punch-shot situation is into a headwind. The lower trajectory allows your ball to maintain its flight pattern without ballooning and falling short of your target.

How to do it
You can hit a punch shot with any iron. (Plan for a loss in distance equal to one club.) Your primary goal is to get your clubface as square to your target as possible at impact with your weight firmly on your left side. It's a 3/4 swing, which is easier to produce than a full one. Here are the specifics to keep your ball low when you have to.
—**John Dahl**

Two musts: Weight forward, hands forward.

Address
Play the ball slightly back of center and forward press your hands so they're in line with your left thigh. Pre-set about 70 percent of your weight on your front foot.

Lead the club back to the ball with your turn.

Swing
Make a 75 percent backswing with a tiny shift of weight to your right foot. On the downswing, use more body turn than arm swing to bring the club back to the ball.

Don't stop turning and keep your club low.

Impact
Keep your left wrist firm at impact and your clubhead low to the ground as you swing into your follow-through. This ensures that you won't add loft and hit the ball too high.

PLAN YOUR APPROACH
How to be aggressive while avoiding costly mistakes

How to Attack When the Pin Is Back

Here's your plan to get it close

The situation
125-yard par 3, pin cut in the middle of the third tier on a green that slopes back to front. A stiff 20-mph wind is in your face.

20-mph wind

THE TOP 100 SAY

48%—Play for the back tier with a punch/knockdown shot

38%—Play a safe low shot to the middle of the green and let your putter do the rest.

14%—When's the last time you practiced a punch? Make your regular swing and play to the middle of the green— always the smartest play.

If you're an aggressive player...
Hit a knockdown to the pin

Club selection: If the card says the hole is 125 yards and the pin is back, figure you have 135 to the hole. The general rule for playing into the wind is one more club for every 10 mph. So if you normally hit a 9-iron from 135 yards, you should drop down to a 7-iron here. But since you're going to play a knockdown, drop down one more club to a 6-iron.
Swing tip: Trust that you have enough club and make a three-quarter swing back and through. Lead the club into impact with the shaft leaning toward the target.
Target: Aim at the middle of the second tier. Your knockdown shot should skip forward to the third tier before it grabs.

"Ben Hogan said, 'Never hit a high ball to a back pin.' That's great advice."
—Charlie Sorrell

If you're not confident with the knockdown shot...
Hit a regular full shot to the middle tier

Club selection: Go up two clubs for the wind and make your normal swing. If you pure it you might reach the back tier. If you don't, you'll still have an excellent chance of a two-putt par.
Swing tip: Forget the wind and make a relaxed swing. Don't try to "power" the ball or juice up your tempo, because even if you pure it you'll just create more backspin and the ball will fly higher (and shorter) into the wind.
Target: Even though you're planning to land your ball on the middle tier of the green, you should still aim for the top of the pin.

"How many clubs is a 20 mph wind worth to you? Most golfers come up short even without wind. Ask yourself: can you hit the club you select over the green? If not, then you aren't swinging enough club."
—Shawn Humphries

If you tend to slice or hook your irons...

Play a low shot to the middle tier, because low shots spin less.
You need to keep spin to a minimum because wind exacerbates backspin, and if you hit your normal shot you'll end up short.

Club selection: Plus two for the wind.
Swing tip: You don't need a pure knockdown—just something slightly lower to keep the ball under the wind. Think of hitting a long chip—play the ball back of center and think of squaring the clubface with your body, not your hands. That means rotating your hips and shoulders to the left of your target from the top of your backswing to well past impact.
Target: Center of the green.

"If you tend to cut or hook the ball, wind can spell disaster, especially on a tee shot on a par 3. A headwind magnifies any curving ball flight, so controlling the shot shape is a critical factor. An intentional punch is ideal in this situation because it's easier to control both the distance and direction and it keeps spin to a minimum."
—Keith Lyford

Stop Leaving Yourself the Wrong First Putt

For more one- and two-putts, think about splitting the green into quadrants

The fat parts of the green may look tempting, but the putts they leave can be killers.

The situation
You have a decent lie and you're in definite scoring range, but you're not sure if you should shoot straight for the flagstick.

The common mistake
You play to the fat part of the green to avoid trouble, but this puts you in three-putt territory.

The right play
Before you set up for any approach shot, take the extra time to divide the green into numbered quadrants, using the flagstick as the midpoint. Then examine each quadrant to determine which one is the most likely to leave you with the easiest uphill putt.

How to do it
When you divide the photo above into quadrants, you're left with two large areas to the left of the pin and two smaller ones to the right. Moving clockwise from the back right, number the quadrants 1, 2, 3 and 4. At first glance, you might be tempted to aim at quadrant 3 or 4, but each of those will leave you with a downhill putt, and you can't be aggressive when putting downhill. Quadrant 1 will also leave you a downhill putt, so you're left with quadrant 2. This may be a tougher shot, but from inside 100 yards you should be able to get your ball there and have the easiest putt on the green: straight uphill.
—**Michael Breed**

Don't Hold Back

You have a better chance of hitting the ball solidly by swinging with your normal tempo rather than trying to hold back and swing easy.

A typical green is about 30 yards deep, so if your yardage is 150 to the center, that means 135 is your number to the front of the green. Assuming there isn't a water hazard guarding the front, choose the club that gets you to that 135-140 distance and make a confident swing through impact.
—**Keith Lyford**

When you're between clubs, hit the shorter one at full speed to the front portion of the green.

SPECIAL PLAYS

You won't always get a perfect lie at your favorite short-iron distance. Here's how to adjust for slope and hit close to the target from anywhere inside 100 yards.

INSTRUCTION

How to Hit From Any Distance

Change your club, not your tempo

After extensive testing and research, I discovered that the best way to control distance is with the length of your backswing. Make it shorter for short shots and longer for long shots, all with the same rhythm and a full follow-through. Imagine a clock, with the 12:00 position above your head. When your hands reach 12:00, you're set for full power. The 10:30 position generates 80 percent of your full-swing distance, while the 9:00 and 7:30 positions produce 60 percent and 40 percent distances, respectively.

The 7:30, 9:00 and 10:30 swings, paired with four wedges in your set, give you 12 unique distances. This system guards against the biggest short-shot killer of them all: deceleration. Find the yardage, select the club/swing combination, and pull the trigger.

—**Dave Pelz**

Groove three backswings (7.30, 9.00 and 10.30) and everything in between becomes easy.

64° XW	60° LW
55 YARDS	**70** YARDS
55° SW	49° PW
85 YARDS	**100** YARDS

64° XW	60° LW
42 YARDS	**53** YARDS
55° SW	49° PW
64 YARDS	**75** YARDS

64° XW	60° LW
28 YARDS	**35** YARDS
55° SW	49° PW
43 YARDS	**53** YARDS

10.30
9.00
7.30

Target Practice

How to attack a tucked pin

The situation

You're in the fairway, inside 100 yards, but here the pin is tucked behind a bunker in the back-right corner of the green. Should you take dead aim and play to the flag or hit the safer shot toward the open portion of the green?

The solution

Consider the following:

Your lie
• If the ball rests on an upslope, it's easier to hit it high and make it stop quickly. **Go for it!**
• A downslope makes it tough to get enough loft on your shot. **Play it safe**

Swing length
• Can you reach the hole with a full swing? If so, you'll be able to generate more spin. **Go for it!**
• If the distance requires a less-than-full swing, your control will be less precise. **Play it safe**

Your typical miss
• If you tend to miss your wedge shots long, the front bunker won't come in to play. **Go for it!**
• If you typically miss short, you bring the bunker into play. **Play it safe**
—**Don Kotnik**

INSTRUCTION

Make Clean Contact From Sidehill Lies

Save strokes from uphill and downhill situations with this easy foot move

The problem

You have trouble making solid contact and staying in balance when your lie isn't perfectly flat. From these lies, you tend to lean into the hill, which almost always results in an inconsistent array of fat and thin shots.

The solution

The secret to avoiding this error is to make sure that your shoulders match the slope of the hill. Easier said than done—after all, how do you make your shoulders even with the slope of a hill without tipping over? The answer lies in the position of your downhill foot.

Flaring your left foot positions the bottom of your swing arc at the ball.

A flared right foot will give you more freedom to swing from an uphill lie.

Downhill lie

Club selection
A downhill lie subtracts loft from your shot, so you should take a more lofted club when you're hitting a ball down a slope.

Ball position
Play the ball in the middle of your stance or even slightly toward your back, or uphill, foot.

Stance
Flare your left foot about 45 degrees. This gives your left side a more stable platform, so you can tilt your shoulders to match the slope and swing without losing your balance.

Swing
Make your regular swing with your normal tempo.

Flare your left foot and play the ball back for clean contact on a downhill.

Uphill lie

Club selection
An uphill lie adds loft to your shot, so you should take a less lofted club when you're hitting a ball up a slope.

Ball position
For an uphill lie, move your ball an inch or two farther toward your uphill foot than you normally would.

Stance
Flare your right foot about 45 degrees to even out your stance from this lie and position the the bottom of your swing arc at the ball at so you don't slam your club into the hill.

Swing
Make your regular swing with your normal tempo.

Play the ball forward and flare your right foot for clean contact on an uphill.

QUICK TIP
When the ball is above your feet, take more club and choke down. When the ball is below your feet, try to maintain posture.

Even the best players on Tour miss five to six greens a round. Unlike you, however, they rarely make five or six bogeys. A solid short game turns potential disaster holes into easy pars.

SECTION 6

YOUR SHORT GAME

Whether it's an approach to a par 5 or a greenside chip, here's how to get it close

Some days your full-swing shots just can't miss; other times you can't hit greens even from a perfect lie with your favorite club in your hands. That's when your short game shows how important it is to keeping your scores down. Those mild-mannered chips, pitches and lobs make up for poor shots in a hurry, taking you from parts unknown to a comfortable spot next to the pin with swings that rarely go above knee height.

There are thousands of ways to get the ball close from short range, but instead of confusing you with a multitude of setup and swing options, this section breaks down your short game into five simple shots: bump-and-run chips; high, medium and low pitches; and lob shots. Mastering these basic short-game plays arms you with enough shotmaking options to tackle anything the course throws at you during your round. Plus, by the time you have these short shots down pat, you'll understand the adjustments you need to make when facing more difficult situations.

Short swings are easy to learn. So if you struggle to get the ball close, pay attention to the Top 100's advice and prepare to see an instant improvement in your scores.

5 THINGS YOU'LL LEARN IN THIS SECTION

- The right way to set up for a chip so that your club automatically catches the ball clean
- How to vary your club selection to produce the correct amount of carry and roll for any situation
- How to pitch the ball close to the pin from the fairway—and even add spin if you want it
- How to pitch higher or lower so you can attack the pin regardless of what's between you and the hole
- The essential keys for pulling off flops and lob shots

CHIP IT CLOSER

Here's how to make those tough little shots from off the green a piece of cake and get up-and-down every time

How to Hit the Perfect Chip

Borrow from your putting stroke to create solid short shots

As with most shots, you'll hit better chips if your setup position is correct. The goal of your chipping address position is to situate your body, arms, hands and club to create a descending blow without chunking the clubhead into the ground, or striking the ball with the leading edge of the clubface. Your setup and technique are correct if your impact position looks like this.

KEY MOVE

CLUBHEAD LOW
Compare the height of the ball with the height of the clubhead: The ball is high and the clubhead is still very low to the ground. This proves that a downward strike—not an upward flip—gets the ball rolling up the clubface and into the air.

TOE CLOSED
Although your hands should be passive and your left wrist straight, they do need to rotate so that the club turns over on its heel through impact. Try to smoothly rotate the toe of the cub toward your target (don't jerk it) as you swing through the impact area.

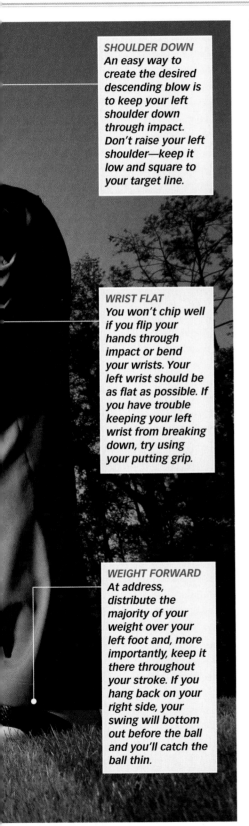

SHOULDER DOWN
An easy way to create the desired descending blow is to keep your left shoulder down through impact. Don't raise your left shoulder—keep it low and square to your target line.

WRIST FLAT
You won't chip well if you flip your hands through impact or bend your wrists. Your left wrist should be as flat as possible. If you have trouble keeping your left wrist from breaking down, try using your putting grip.

WEIGHT FORWARD
At address, distribute the majority of your weight over your left foot and, more importantly, keep it there throughout your stroke. If you hang back on your right side, your swing will bottom out before the ball and you'll catch the ball thin.

INSTRUCTION

How to Set Up for Solid Chips

Get the heel of the club up and the handle forward for a solid, consistent chip stroke

Raise your wedge on its toe so it sits like a putter.

Step 1

Aim the clubface at your target, and then raise the club slightly on its toe. This gives you a more upright lie, which makes your chip swing more of a putting stroke. A putting stroke is easier to control because it moves straight back and through. A flatter lie demands you swing the club on an arc.

Step 2

Move the handle of your club two inches farther toward the target than the front edge of the ball. This de-lofts the clubhead and promotes the downward strike that you're looking for. You can use any wedge with this technique, and even your 8- or 9-iron will work.

Step 3

The butt of your club should point a couple of inches left of the center of your body. Make sure that your shoulders are square to the target line and your weight is over your left foot, and then play the ball off your right big toe.

Step 4

Move the club with your arms and shoulders while keeping your hands and wrists quiet and your weight on your left side. As you swing through the hitting zone, you should feel as though you're striking down on the ball while gently closing the clubface.
—Todd Sones

INSTRUCTION

Make a "y" to Chip It Close

You'll catch the ball clean with the handle forward

Fault

You hit your chips fat so they never get close to the flag, or you blade them over the green.

Fix

As you take your address, make sure you set most of your weight over your left foot and move the handle of the club forward. Notice that when you do this your arms and clubshaft form a lower case "y".

Establishing this y and keeping it intact during your chipping motion will allow you to come down sharply on the ball and catch it clean before your clubhead makes contact with the turf. Try to "trap" the ball between your clubface and the ground at impact. This will keep your hands forward of the ball and ensure proper contact.

—Steve Bosdosh

Make a "y" at address...

...and maintain it during your swing.

How to Chip From Every Lie

Let your backswing do the work for you

The problem

You assume that one swing will get the job done for every chipping situation. In reality, however, you need at least two: One for lies in the rough and another for tight lies. Here's how to match your swing to the situation and leave your chips closer to the hole.

How to find the right chip plane

Spread some balls around a chipping green, making sure you're left with many different lies. Then, vary your technique to match each shot. If it's available, place a mirror behind you and check that your backswing works to the inside on normal chips and outside on chips from the rough. If you're still struggling, exaggerate each move until you get the results you want.
—Brian Mogg

Swing inside from a tight lie

Your goal is to sweep the ball off the turf with a rounded swing. Imagine a shaft stuck in the ground behind your ball and on your target line. Take the clubhead away to the inside of the shaft with very little wrist hinge, as though you were attempting a long putt. Do the same on your forward swing, and release the clubhead toward the target while keeping your hands at thigh height.

Swing outside from the rough

When your ball is sitting down, swing your clubhead outside the shaft on your backswing and hinge your wrists aggressively to get the club up. (Think "low hands, high clubhead.") On your downswing, drop your arms toward the ground and across the ball (left of the target) without releasing your hands. This allows you to dig deep and pop the ball up without fear of catching it thin.

Keep your hands low.

TIP *Since this is a shallow swing, expect minimal spin and more roll once the ball hits the turf.*

Quickly hinge the club up.

TIP *You'll generate extra loft using this technique, so plan to fly the ball at least three quarters of the distance to the flagstick.*

Land the Ball in the Right Spot

Use the Tour's 25 percent rule

Working with CompuSport, a biomechanics research firm, I studied 30 PGA Tour pros hitting shots inside 100 yards. On short shots from just off the green, they consistently landed the ball a quarter of the way from the front edge of the green to the flag. So, if the hole was eight paces from the front, they dropped the ball two paces on.

When they needed more or less flight, the pros changed clubs but kept the landing spot a quarter of the way on. If the green sloped away, they took a more lofted club and used the extra height to counter the faster surface. If the green ran uphill, they used a less lofted club for a hotter roll. But 25 percent was the Tour's golden rule.

—Fred Griffin

QUICK TIP
Leave the flagstick in when chipping. Even if you don't hit the pin dead center, it will keep more of your shots in the hole.

Follow the Tour's lead and land the ball a quarter of the way from the front edge to the flagstick.

How to Roll It to Tap-In Range

Keep the ball on the ground when you have lots of green in front of you

Unless you have a Tour-level short game or practice flop shots regularly, forget about hoisting one of those high-lofted shots to the hole—it's unnecessary and ups the odds for a miscue. Even if you catch it clean, it will have big-time backspin, so if you land on a slope it will roll back down.

Whenever there's lots of green between you and the hole, get the ball rolling as soon as you can. Chip the ball onto the green and send it toward the cup like it's a putt. It's a lot easier to make solid contact with the short swing you'll need, and your distance control will be a lot better, too.
—Jim Murphy

How to pick the right chip stick

● *A sand-wedge chip will roll the same distance as it flies (a 1:1 ratio). A pitching-wedge chip will roll twice as far as it flies (1:2); a 9-iron is 1:3 and so on.*

● *Based on the 25% Rule, if there's 40 feet between you and the pin, an 9-iron is the perfect choice since the shot needs 10 feet of carry and 30 feet of roll.*

A bump-and-run shot is more reliable than a high-flying lob.

Should I Chip With One Club or Many?

If I'm looking to have a great short game, should I always hit bump-and-runs with a 7- or 8-iron or should I use a single club, such as a wedge, all the time?

You need two basic shots—the bump-and-run, and the lofted chip. The bump-and-run is the best for dry, firm ground because it's difficult to predict how a higher shot will bounce once it hits the ground. You're better off keeping it low and letting it roll like a putt. Wet and soft greens demand a wedge so you can fly the shot almost all the way to the hole. You don't need to alter your trajectory too much. Instead, lengthen or shorten your motion depending on the carry distance.
—Donald Crawley

Map Out Your Attack

If you can't judge the distance, play to a zone

When you chip, picture the green divided into four sections. Zone 1 is closest to you, Zones 2 and 3 are in the middle, and Zone 4 is the farthest away. No matter where the hole is located, always land the ball in Zone 1 and make it roll to the hole. What club will do the job? If your ball lies just off the green, use this system:

● **Finish in Zone 1:** Sand or lob wedge
● **Roll to Zone 2:** 9-iron or pitching wedge
● **Roll to Zone 3:** 8- or 9-iron
● **Roll to Zone 4:** 7- or 8-iron
—Eden Foster

Get on Your Left Side to Chip It Stiff

A proper weight shift will guarantee better contact from tight lies

The problem
When you face a chip from a tight lie you fear skulling it so you hit it fat.

The solution
Pretend you're balanced on a small seesaw. At address, the seesaw should tilt to the left. This means your weight is perfectly positioned so you can hit down on the ball and catch it clean.

How to practice it
Hit chips with an empty plastic water bottle under your right foot. Play the ball slightly back of center, and use the bottle to remind you to shift your weight over to your left leg. Shifting your weight forward and keeping it there during your stroke correctly positions the bottom of your swing arc at the back of the ball—you won't be able to hit the ground behind the ball if you try.

—Bill Forrest

If you chipped standing on a seesaw the right side would be up.

WRONG!

Simply shifting your hips to the left won't get your weight on your left side where it needs to be for clean contact.

RIGHT!

Practice chipping with a small plastic bottle under your right foot to remind you to set your weight forward and keep it there.

DRILL

How to Catch Every Chip Clean

Use this simple drill to play perfect little shots

Fault

You try to lift the ball into the air and end up blading it across the green. Solid chips are the result of hitting down into the back of the ball, not trying to lift it up.

Fix

Here's a drill that will produce the kind of chips you dream about—unless it's those blue corn dealies. You'll need to hit the snack aisle for those.

Balance a club on the top of a water bottle as shown (it's easier than it looks), and place the ball 12 inches behind the middle of the grip. Make your chip stroke without knocking the shaft off the bottle [photo right]. You'll need to descend into the ball and keep your clubhead low to the ground after impact. If you try to scoop the ball or allow the club to pass your hands [photo above], you'll send the club and the bottle flying.

—Glenn Deck

Swing down, not up, to avoid a game of pickup sticks.

DRILL

How to Chip Without Yipping

Be aggressive without hitting it too hard

The next time you face a chip shot, think about your stroke being SAD—Short, Aggressive and Down. The enemies of good chipping are LPU: Long, Passive and Up. Do any of those and you'll CSC—Chunk, Skull or Chili. So here's how you can be SAD about your chipping game in 10 minutes.

Pull the clubhead down to the ball with your left hand.

Step 1

With your pitching wedge or 9-iron, set up with a narrow stance and play the ball about midway between your heels. Lay a second club on the ground an inch outside your right foot as shown. The idea is to swing over this club on the way back and down to the ball.

Step 2

Swing back until your hands are about even with your right pocket. This is all you need—any longer and you'll decelerate on the downswing to compensate.

Step 3

Pull the club aggressively down to impact with your left hand. Your wrists and hands should feel firm—that's how you know you didn't try to scoop at the ball. You'll make a short follow-through and see your ball track to the hole.

—John Elliott, Jr.

Feel a firm left wrist at impact.

PITCH LIKE A PRO

You hit 20- to 50-yard shots more than you think—
here's how to pull them off with razor-sharp precision

INSTRUCTION

How to Pitch It Close

Keep your hands low and in to hit laser-like wedges from the fairway

The situation
You have a medium-length pitch of 50 yards from a tight, slightly downhill fairway lie.

The usual mistake
Flipping the clubhead underneath the ball in an attempt to create more loft. The result is often a thin, bladed shot or a chili-dip.

Keep your hands tight to your body as you swing through impact.

How to get the technique

Like you've read, you should lead with the handle of the club, not the head. More importantly, keep your clubhead low and tight to your body as you rotate through the shot *[below right]*. The closer the handle is to your body, the easier it is to hold your wrist angles through impact.

The key to avoiding the flip is to use the opposite end of the club than what seems natural, that is, the grip instead of the clubhead. By pulling the butt of the handle in and up to your left, you will turn to square the clubface and drop the clubhead down to the ball. Turn your body—not your hands—and just let the ball get in the way of your rotation.

WRONG!

RIGHT!

Pull the handle in toward your body, not away from it.

DRILL

Knuckles to the Ground

As you swing through, you should feel as if you're trying to scrape your knuckles along the ground. This sensation will lower the shaft and bring your hands inside, making it nearly impossible to scoop. You can practice this by hitting half-shots, starting with your hands at thigh height. Think about maintaining the relationship between your hands and the clubhead as you swing forward, keeping your hands close to the ground. Pull—don't push—and you'll hit the ball solidly every time.
—**Rick McCord**

Point your knuckles down...

...and scrape them against the ground.

5 More Keys to Solid Pitching

1 Narrow your stance from your normal iron setup so your feet are slightly less than shoulder-width apart.

2 Play the ball in the center of your stance. Move it slightly forward of center for a high, soft-landing shot and back for a lower shot.

3 Allow the length of the shot to dictate the length of your swing. The longer the shot, the longer you should swing your arms back and through.

4 Feel like the clubface is sliding across the inside of the ball, not hitting the back of it. An inside approach will keep your right palm facing out to the right, adding loft.

5 Don't limit your follow-through. The length of your swing is not as important as its speed. Let your finish be dictated by the rate of acceleration: the faster your swing, the longer your finish.
—**Rick McCord**

INSTRUCTION

Pitch It High or Low

Here are three shots that travel the same distance on three different trajectories

Not all pitches are equal—sometimes you need more loft to carry an obstacle or to fly the ball onto an upper tier, while other situations require you to hit a low runner so you can use the contour of the green to snuggle your ball up to the hole. So to get it as close as possible on any pitch shot, you must know how to alter the trajectory of the ball. All you need to do is change your setup and swing length to produce the desired height. Follow the chart below to become an instant shotmaker from 20 yards.
—**Bill Moretti**

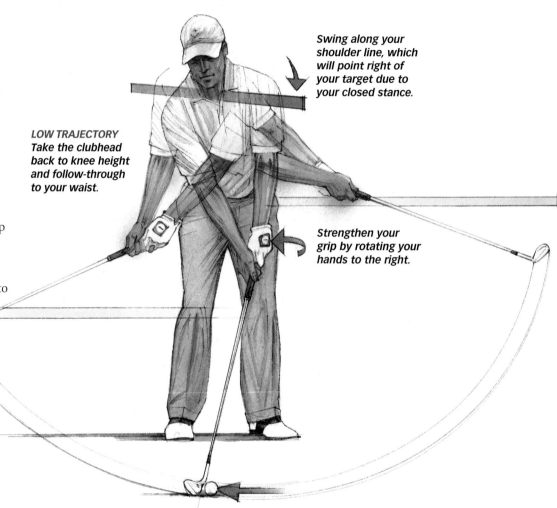

Swing along your shoulder line, which will point right of your target due to your closed stance.

LOW TRAJECTORY
Take the clubhead back to knee height and follow-through to your waist.

Strengthen your grip by rotating your hands to the right.

Pitching adjustments (20-yard shot)

	Low shot	Medium shot	High shot
Grip	Stronger (hands rotated to the right)	Standard	Weak (hands rotated to the left)
Stance	Closed shoulders; ball back of center	Square shoulders; ball middle of stance	Open shoulders; ball forward of center
Shaft lean	Butt end of club at middle of left thigh; hands 4 to 6 inches in front of ball	Butt end of club at middle of left thigh; hands slightly forward of ball	Butt end of club at navel; hands 1 to 3 inches behind ball
Swing length	Knee-high to waist-high	Waist-high to waist-high	Chest-high to waist-high
Swing path	Along shoulder line (right of target due to closed stance)	Along shoulder line	Along shoulder line (left of target due to open stance)

Align the lead edge of your wedge just below the equator of the ball so you can reach for the ball and catch it crisp.

MEDIUM TRAJECTORY
Square shoulders, hands slightly forward, swing waist to waist.

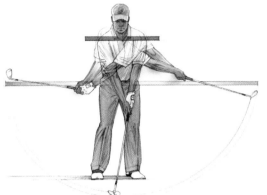

HIGH TRAJECTORY
Weaken grip, open shoulders, swing chest-high to waist-high.

Reach for It!

Try this trick to stop blading your chips

Address the ball in a taller posture and align the leading edge of your club just below the equator of the ball. On your forward stroke, stay loose and let your arms lengthen. If you do, your club will correctly bottom out in front of the ball. "Under-reaching" at address like this gives you a better margin for error to create crisp contact.
—Tim Mahoney

DRILL

How to be Pitcher Perfect

Hit the shot with your body, not your hands

The problem

Poor pitch shots result from overactive hands and wrists, so keep them calm and instead pitch the ball with your body. Here's a drill that will teach you to rotate your upper and lower body completely through the shot and produce a more consistent launch angle and extra distance.

The solution

Place a dowel that's at least 24" (or longer) in the hole on top of your grip and lean the shaft forward at address so the dowel is left of your front hip. Then try to pitch the ball by pulling the club through impact with your body turn, not by flipping your wrists.
—Anne Cain

QUICK TIP
For a smoother pitch swing, use a weak grip, with the Vs formed by your thumb and forefinger pointed at your chin.

NO!
Don't stop turning or get handsy.

YOU'RE DOING IT WRONG IF...
The dowel smacks the left side of your torso in your forward-swing.

YES!
Keep your hands passive—pull them through impact with your body turn.

YOU'RE DOING IT RIGHT IF...
You pitch the ball cleanly and the dowel stays left of your body throughout your motion.

Soften Up Your Pitches

How to hit it higher and land it softer

The situation

You're faced with a tricky pitch with an obstacle between you and the pin. You need loft and pinpoint distance control or you won't get up and down.

The standard play

Hit a high, floating lob shot with your 60-degree wedge or a lower pitch with tons of spin to get your ball to stop after a single hop. Problem is, the lob shot is a high-risk alternative and most recreational players can't generate the spin needed to stop the ball on a dime.

The better play

The Super Soft Pitch—a simple shot that adds extra loft to your everyday pitching motion. You'll get a high shot that stops near where it lands without having to make the perfect lob.

—Donald Crawley

How to play the Super Soft Pitch

The key to hitting the Super Soft Pitch is to pre-set your body in the correct impact position at address. This helps you strike the ball with the right amount of loft. In the past, you've pitched the ball either too low or too high because your poor impact position either added or subtracted loft from your clubface.

Setup

Sole either your 56- or 60-degree wedge on the turf with the face square and pointing directly at your target. (There's no need to open it—that only creates extra bounce and increases the potential for thin contact.)

SHOULDERS
Make sure your shoulders are level and that your arms hang straight down. Ease up on your grip pressure—this shot requires soft hands.

BALL POSITION
Play the ball just back of center and lean the shaft forward. (Be careful not to close the clubface.) Your grip should line up with your sternum about an inch in front of the ball with your weight favoring your front foot.

Swing

Make your backswing by swinging your arms and chest away from the ball using soft hands and an easy hinge of your wrists. Your swing path should feel pretty straight, but with a slight turn so that the toe of the clubhead points straight up once your hands reach knee height.

DOWNSWING
Stop your backswing just as your hands pass your right knee. On your downswing, turn toward the target and unhinge your wrists so that you return the clubhead, shaft and weight to the same position they were in at address. When you do this correctly, your club will descend into the bottom of the ball with the correct loft.

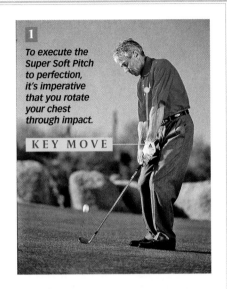

1

To execute the Super Soft Pitch to perfection, it's imperative that you rotate your chest through impact.

KEY MOVE

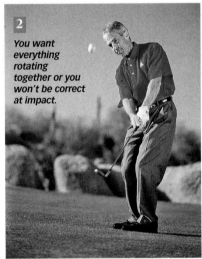

2

You want everything rotating together or you won't be correct at impact.

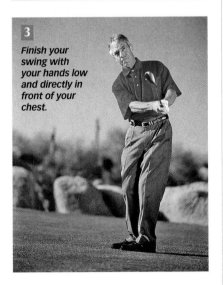

3

Finish your swing with your hands low and directly in front of your chest.

INSTRUCTION

How to Make Your Pitches Bite

Accelerate then stop to get the check, please

If your pitches fly straight, but land on the green without any spin and run past the hole, use the keys below to help the ball land on your target then grab the green harder than a miner's handshake.

—Brian Mogg

QUICK TIP
The faster you accelerate then stop, the more the ball will run up the face and grab in the grooves. That groove-grab adds spin.

Step 1
On your backswing, point your thumbs at the sky and the butt of the club at the ground.

Step 2
Come down sharply into the ball to get it rolling up the clubface.

Step 3
Once you feel impact, stop your hands abruptly at waist height and keep them and your club low.

CHECKPOINT

For Sale: Extra Spin

The right gear makes for easy checkups

Three tests by Golf Laboratories show that a rusty wedge and a clean, high-spin ball can give you thousands of extra revolutions of spin (www.golflabs.com).

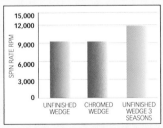

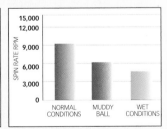

UNFINISHED BUSINESS
New chromed and unfinished 56° sand wedges (same make and model) produced similar rpms, but the same unfinished wedge used over three seasons sent spin rates off the charts.

SPIN BALL WIZARDS
Does a true high-spin ball (like the Titleist Pro V1) spin more than a pure distance model (like the Top-Flite Extreme Distance) off the same wedge? The results speak for themselves.

CLEAN UP YOUR ACT
Mud on the ball reduced spin by 33%, and water (simulated by dunking the club and ball) cut the spin rate by 49%. So if you play under the lift, clean and place rule, take advantage of it!

HOW TO LOB IT

Sometimes you need to carry an obstacle and fly the ball all the way to the flag. These tricks will turn you into a major flopper.

Flip the club past your hands to lob the ball high from rough.

Get Wristy to Lob It From Rough

On this shot, it's OK to make an early release

The mistake you should make

On most shots, wristy impact is a recipe for disaster. However, when you have to pop the ball high and soft, you actually want to flip your wrists.

How to commit it

Set up with a slightly open stance and play the ball slightly back of center. Take your regular pitch backswing, but as you come back down, slow your arms and hips (something you do anyway if you often muff pitch shots) and quickly break your wrists through impact. Don't allow your arms to pass your body. If it helps to think of folding your left wrist or bowing your right, do it. At the finish, your right hand should hide your left. While this is the opposite of traditional short-game advice, it's exactly what you need in this situation.

Why it works

Flipping the club past your hands increases the effective loft of the clubface. So you get extra height on the shot that you normally wouldn't get if you adhered to the standard advice of keeping your hands ahead of the club at impact. Plus, deceleration is common on short swings, so you don't even have to practice this shot. The technique works with any of your wedges, but to hit the ball extra high and help it land soft (don't expect much spin with this technique), use your lob wedge.
—Eden Foster

Don't try it when...

Your lie is tight. The wrist-break flop shot requires perfect timing and has zero margin of error from a tight lie, so unless you have a fluffy lie in greenside rough, don't attempt this shot.

1
With your most lofted wedge, make your normal backswing and fully hinge your wrists.

2
As you approach impact, apply the brakes to your arms and step on the gas with your wrists.

3
Use your wrists to flip the clubhead under the ball and past your hands.

CHECKPOINT

Stay Down to Loft the Ball Up

Keep your focus on the point of impact well after the ball is on its way

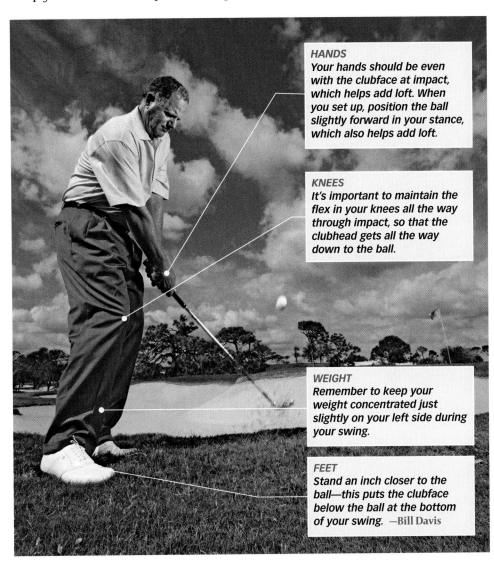

HANDS
Your hands should be even with the clubface at impact, which helps add loft. When you set up, position the ball slightly forward in your stance, which also helps add loft.

KNEES
It's important to maintain the flex in your knees all the way through impact, so that the clubhead gets all the way down to the ball.

WEIGHT
Remember to keep your weight concentrated just slightly on your left side during your swing.

FEET
Stand an inch closer to the ball—this puts the clubface below the ball at the bottom of your swing. —Bill Davis

INSTRUCTION

Aim for Groove 4

It's the key for lobbing from tight lies

Imagine contacting the ball between the third and fifth grooves up from the bottom of the clubface. This encourages you to make a descending blow, with the shaft leaning forward at impact. Your wrists won't break down, and the ball will climb up the face and into the air.
—Charlie King

Hit down on the ball, making contact on the fourth groove to get the ball rolling up the face.

Getting out of bunkers is very easy if you have the right mind-set and use the proper techniques.

SECTION 7

ESCAPING THE SAND

Bunker shots come in many shapes,
lies and levels of difficulty.
Here's how to play them all.

There's a big gap between the bunker skills seen on Tour and those on display at your local muni. Most recreational golfers approach a sandy lie like the ball is covered in Kryptonite. Pros, on the other hand, thrive in sand, and would rather hit out of a bunker than chip from the rough. Tour players prefer bunker shots compared to other alternatives when they miss the green because (1) it's an easy shot, and (2) it's something they practice regularly. Unless the lie is very difficult, you can expect a top-tier player to get up and down from a bunker two-thirds of the time.

The goal of this section is to close this gap and help you become more familiar with sand shots and the relatively simple technique needed to get the ball out and onto the green. How simple? It's the only shot where it's okay for you to miss the ball. Plus, the club you use most often from sand comes with a special design trait—bounce—that makes blasting out just that much easier.

The instruction on the following pages will help you conquer any bunker lie imaginable, including the ones that typically send your scores through the roof. Soon, you'll look forward to hitting from sand—just like the pros do.

5 THINGS YOU'LL LEARN IN THIS SECTION

- How to escape greenside bunkers on your first swing
- Adjustments you need to make for different lies and conditions to blast the ball close
- How to take the right amount of sand and correctly use the bounce on your wedges
- How to add height and spin to stop your sand shots from short distances
- Setup and swing keys to handle the most nasty and terrifying bunker situations

The Most Difficult Shot in Golf

In a recent *GOLF Magazine* survey, we asked what shot gives you the most trouble.

40-yard bunker shot: 33%   **Approach shot over water: 22%**

Other: 26%   **Half-wedge shot: 19%**

Even Tour pros struggle with the 40-yard sand shot, getting up and down less than a third of the time. By comparison, the 2006 PGA Tour average for getting up and down from a greenside bunker was 55 percent.

"On long bunker shots, drop down to an 9- or 8-iron and make a U-shaped swing (instead of the V-shaped swing you make in greenside bunkers). Hit the sand about an inch behind the ball and follow through. Your ball will still ride out on a cushion of sand, but the less-lofted club and rounder swing will fly the ball to the green."
—Dr. Jim Suttie

BUNKER-SHOT BASICS
Proven techniques for getting out of sand traps on the first try—every time

How to Blast It Close From the Sand

Follow these three easy steps for foolproof escapes from normal lies

12:00

Keep your legs wide and quiet.

Attack from the inside.

Step 1:
With the flagstick representing 12:00 on a clock face, open up your stance just slightly, so your feet, hips and shoulders are pointing to 11:30. Aim the leading edge of your sand wedge at the flag.

Step 2:
Spread your feet two inches wider than normal. A wider stance helps quiet your legs so you can correctly swing more with your arms. A wider stance makes it easier to repeat your swing and control your clubhead.

Step 3:
These adjustments will help you attack the ball from the inside with the clubface square to the target, so not only will you get out of the bunker, the ball will fly at your target.
—Scott Sackett

CHECKPOINT

Is Your Divot in the Right Place?

This simple drill gives you the answer

A perfect bunker swing enters the sand about two to three inches behind the ball, skims a half-inch to an inch under the surface, then emerges about three inches in front of where the ball rested. The clubhead never touches the ball itself. The sand carries the ball up and out.

To see if you're doing it correctly, draw parallel lines in the sand about six inches apart, drop a ball between them and make your swing. Check the guide at right to see if you're entering the sand too early, entering the sand too late or taking too large of a divot.

—**Paul Marchand**

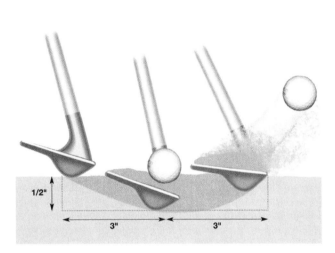

1/2" 3" 3"

Imagine a cheese danish with the ball in the center of the cheese, and simply knock out the entire danish. That's how big your divot should be.

—**Steve Bosdosh**

Check your track marks

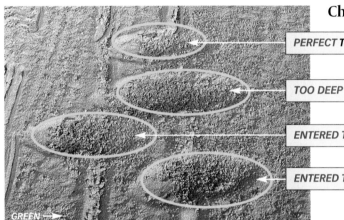

*PERFECT **The club never touched the ball.***

*TOO DEEP **This one was left in the bunker.***

*ENTERED TOO EARLY **Left it in the bunker again.***

*ENTERED TOO LATE **This was bladed over the green.***

GREEN →

DRILL

How to Use Your Wedge's Bounce

That chunk of metal on the bottom of your wedge is the key to hitting great bunker shots

On most iron shots from the fairway, the leading edge of the club touches the ground first, and then digs into the turf. **On shots from the bunker, the first thing that should enter the sand must be the trailing edge of your wedge.** This allows the bounce (the fat, protruding hunk of metal on the bottom of the club) to glide the club through the sand rather than digging into it and stopping the forward momentum of your clubhead.

Bury a two-by-four that's at least 12 inches long in the sand so that the top is even with the sand's surface. Pile about an inch of sand on the board and place a ball on top. Make your normal bunker swing and try to erase the sand from the board, making contact an inch or two behind the ball. Try to get the pocket of sand to reach the green. This drill familiarizes you with how bounce feels in action, and also trains you to take divots that are the correct size and depth.

—**Scott Sackett**

Swipe sand off a board to practice taking the right size divot.

What to do When You're Up Against the Lip

This bunker buster will do the trick

The situation

Your ball has stopped in the sand a foot or so below the lip.

The solution

Because the ball is sitting on such an extreme upslope, don't feel as though you need to use the most lofted club in your bag—your sand wedge, pitching wedge or even your 9-iron will work just fine. And since the ball is too low on the face for you to keep both feet out of the bunker, you're going to have to get dirty.

Start by stepping down into the bunker so that your back foot is as far below the ball as the ball is below the lip. This will effectively put the ball in the center of your stance. Open the clubface, aim right of your target, and lower your right shoulder to get your shoulders more even with the slope. Then take the club back on a steep, V-shaped path and bring it down hard into the sand just below the ball, driving the heel of the club into the hill. There's no need to make a conscious follow-through—the concussion of the club hitting the sand is what drives the ball out and onto the green.

—Jason Carbone

Drive the heel of your club into the sand to get the ball out.

Plant your right foot as far below the ball as the ball is below the lip.

Drop your right shoulder so your shoulders ar even with the slope.

How to Stop It Quick From the Sand

No green? No problem!

The situation
You have a good lie in a greenside bunker, but you've short-sided yourself and have just a few paces of green between you and the flag. You need a high, soft sand shot that stops on a dime.

The solution
Here are four easy steps to make it sit.

Use your most-lofted wedge and a lot of wrist action to hit the ball high from short distance.

Step 1
Select your most-lofted wedge. Position the ball slightly forward in your stance and move the handle of the club in-line with your right thigh to add extra loft to the clubface.

Step 2
Spread your stance by taking a step out with your right foot and dig both feet into the sand a half-inch for balance. Your shaft should now point just left of the center of your torso.

Step 3
Make sure your shoulder line and shaft line form an angled "T." Your job is to recreate the "T" at impact so that your club enters the sand with the same amount of loft you established at address. Swing your club more with your arms and your wrists, using minimum shoulder movement.

Step 4
Keep your chest pointed down and swing your arms and hands underneath your body. Move onto your left hip through impact to keep the club from releasing past your hands. Try to keep your hands and clubhead low in your follow-through so the clubface stays open.
—**Todd Sones**

A Last Resort: The Drop Shot

Taking your allowable drop might be a better bet than trying to pull off a miracle escape

According to Rule 28 of the USGA Rules of Golf, a player "may deem his ball unplayable at any place on the course except when the ball is in a water hazard." In this case, you have three options, all of which carry a one-stroke penalty:

(a) Play a ball as nearly as possible at the spot from which the original ball was last played.

(b) Drop a ball behind the point where the original ball lay, keeping that point directly between the hole and the spot on which the ball is dropped.

(c) Drop a ball within two club-lengths of the spot where the original ball lay, but not nearer the hole.

If you choose b or c, you must drop the ball within the bunker.

Bury Your Club From Buried Lies

For nasty buried lies, your best bet
is to go pound sand!

The situation

Your ball is three-quarters buried in loose sand toward the upper
part of a steep lip. Even taking a stance won't be easy. You'll have no
trouble swinging the club back, but deep sand and the overhanging
lip will severely limit your follow-through.

The solution

Realistically, you can't do much more to the ball than dislodge it. But
guess what? That's about all you have to do! In fact, you're free to
commit the most common bunker error of all time and quit on the
shot. More good news? You get to make a violent, no-finish swing
and pound that stupid bunker!

How to do it

Step 1: Use whichever of your
wedges has the most bounce and
open the clubface just a bit at
setup. As you finish settling into
your address posture, dig your
back foot deeper in the sand than
your front.

Step 2: Make a full backswing,
then slam the club powerfully into
the sand an inch or two behind
your ball as if you're trying to bury
the clubhead.

Step 3: Don't expect any follow-
through, just a soft rebound effect
as your club emerges lazily from

the sand. Meanwhile your ball
and a half-cup of sand are already
crossing the bunker lip on their
way to the green.

Why it works

The difference between this shot
and one where you quit on it
unintentionally is that, in this
instance, you are accelerating the
clubhead, not decelerating it. As a
result, you can still displace
enough sand to get the ball up
and out of the bunker on an
almost vertical
trajectory.

—Eden Foster

QUICK TIP
If the ball is only
half-buried, use the
same technique, but
close the face and
don't slam the club
into the sand
as hard.

Be sure to
keep most of
your weight
on your left
side.

Anchor your
back foot by
digging it
deeper into the
sand than your
front foot.

There's no need to turn your
right arm over your left after
impact because any follow-
through will be minimal.

The ball can plug,
but it can't hide.

Your clubhead
should literally
burrow into the
sand beneath
the ball.

Blast it close from long range with a club switch, not a swing switch.

INSTRUCTION

Pop and Roll to the Hole

Splash it low to let the ball run on long bunker shots

Fault: You struggle with distance control from bunkers when the hole is clear across the green. The ball either checks up way short, or you skull it way over the green trying to carry it all the way to the hole.

Fix: You need a lower-flying shot that will run. Instead of an open clubface

and stance at address, set them both square to the target line. Try to release the club just like you were hitting a draw—the toe of the club should point up as you follow through and the clubface will rotate closed *[photo above]*. You'll put less spin on the ball and cause it to run once it hits the green.

DRILL

How to practice the low runner from sand

Pick up a handful of sand with your right hand and hold it in front of you in the "address" position. Now throw it over your left shoulder. This is the action your right hand should make after impact, because it closes the clubface to create the lower trajectory. Use this thought and you'll have a new shot to save par.

—**Jerry Mowlds**

Think of tossing the sand over your left shoulder.

INSTRUCTION

3 Steps to Hit a 40-Yard Sand Shot

Time for an old swing with a new club

The situation

You have a decent lie in a bunker, but you're still 40 yards from the flagstick. This shot sends a shiver through even the best sand players because standard blast techniques won't get the ball all the way to the green, and trying to pick the ball clean with your sand wedge is about as easy as picking your teeth with one.

The solution

Before you start thinking "automatic bogey," realize that this difficult shot is actually very easy to pull off. The secret is to keep your sand wedge in your bag and use an iron with less loft and more length, then treat this shot like you would any other bunker escape.

Step 1: Point your toe line to the left of the flagstick and dig in less with your feet.

Step 2: Rotate the clubface open 45 degrees and lean the shaft away from the pin.

Step 3: Make your everyday bunker swing, being careful to swing the club along your toe line, not toward the flagstick. And instead of blasting through the sand like you would from a greenside bunker, take less sand and try to "skid" your club under the ball.

For a shot of 40 yards, use your 9-iron. Drop down to an 8-iron for a 50-yard shot and use a pitching wedge for a 30-yard shot.

Use the same setup and swing for each club/yardage combination. With a little practice you'll have a much easier time pulling off what's considered one of the hardest shots in golf.
—**Dr. Gary Wiren**

How to Play the Three Hardest Bunker Shots

These lies will kill you if you let them. So don't.

Downhill lie

Why it's so hard: It reduces the loft on your wedge in the situation that you need it most. Be clear about what you're trying to accomplish here. If the hole is cut near you, it's unlikely you'll get it close, so just get the ball out. If the hole is on the other side of the green, you have a chance to run it close because this shot will have almost no spin to it.

Set your shoulders parallel to the slope of the bunker, which will shift your weight over your front foot.

Use your most-lofted wedge to counter the de-lofting effect of the slope.

If you can maintain your balance, play the ball opposite your front foot. If that could send you tumbling, play it toward the middle of your stance.

You'll need speed to get the ball up, so make at least a three-quarter backswing.

Have faith in your club. Even de-lofted, it'll still get the ball up. Trying to scoop the ball into the air by flipping your hands is always a bad thing, but in this case it could lead to a total whiff.

Swing down the face of the slope.

Ball above feet

Why it's so hard: A big heap of sand is keeping the ball from rolling to the bottom of the bunker and you have to blast through it. And this baby will immediately fly left of where you're aimed.

An upright swing will bury your club in the sand, so for one of the rare times in the short game, keep your upper body straight up.

Position the ball just forward of center and choke down on the grip to shorten the club so you don't bury it into the hill.

This shot tends to go left, so aim right of your target. The higher the ball is above your feet, the more right you need to aim.

Make a rounded, baseball-type swing to avoid getting the club stuck.

Accelerate aggressively through the shot and try to throw that sand all the way to your target.

Ball below feet

Why it's so hard: If you don't set up to this shot correctly, you'll wind up doing a somersault into the sand. And if the ball is close to the lip of the bunker, you can easily smack the turf.
—Paul Trittler

Bend your knees and lower your rear end to bring the ball within reach.

Spread your feet wider than shoulder width to create a stable base for your swing.

Position the ball forward in your stance, just inside your front foot.

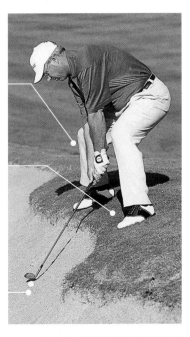

Keep your lower body quiet to maintain balance.

To avoid hitting too far behind the ball, hinge your wrists quickly on your takeaway, then unhinge them as you swing down.

The steeper the slope, the more the ball will want to go right, so aim well left of your target.

TOP 100 SAY

What to Do in Hard or Wet Sand

When the sand is wet...
Add more clubhead speed
Your brain tells you thick wet sand should be more difficult to deal with—you'll get the club stuck in the sand or skull it trying to pick the ball clean. In fact, there's only one adjustment you need to make: swing harder! The sand hasn't changed—it's just heavier, so you need more clubhead speed to displace it. Other than that, keep your technique exactly the same.
—Paul Trittler

When the sand is hard...
Lose your bounce
Hard sand requires two things: (1) a wedge designed with minimal bounce, and (2) the clubface must be wide open when it hits the sand. Less bounce and an open face should allow your club to slide under the ball. When the sand is so shallow that even these adjustments won't work, chip the shot cleanly (ball-first contact). Clean contact requires practice, but it's a good shot to have.
—Dave Pelz

Your scores drop when your putts do likewise.

SECTION 8

HOLING OUT

It all comes down to the most perplexing part of the game—putting. Here's how to get the ball in the hole in far fewer strokes.

I n the end, the object of the game is to get the ball into the hole. While holing a shot isn't your objective on every swing, it is when you're on the green. Here, the cup becomes your true target for the first time on that hole, so pressure builds. If you miss your landing spot in the fairway by a few yards or hit your approach to a section of the green other than which you planned, it's just a miss. Do the same while putting and that miss turns into a stroke lost forever.

The demands of putting are severe, which is ironic since they involve the simplest move you'll make on the course other than getting out of your golf cart. It boils down to that tiny target and the slips, slides, turns, breaks and bumps between it and where your ball lies. There's a lot to overcome, and a lot of questions to be answered. How fast will it go? How hard should I putt it? Is it downhill or flat? Will it go straight or curve left?

There's a school of thought that says it takes years of experience to answer these questions correctly. The Top 100 Teachers disagree, and over the next several pages they'll arm you with everything you need to putt the lights out from any distance. You know what the target is—here are the skills to find it.

5 THINGS YOU'LL LEARN IN THIS SECTION

- How to align your body and aim your putter so your putts start out on the right line
- Find an alternative grip that can compensate for errors in your stroke so your putts still find the hole
- How to study and read greens like a Tour caddie to get the right line and speed
- How to practice and improve your stroke—without getting bored—using the Top 100's best drills
- How to lag putts close so you'll never three-putt again

TOP 100 SAY

How Do You Stack Up Against the Pros?

If you think you already have the magic touch on the greens, try sizing up your game against the true bosses of the mosses—you'll see that you have some work to do. If your putting stats can get even close to these PGA Tour levels, you'll see that solid putting makes up for bad swings from the fairway or the tee box in a hurry.

30.5
Putts per round

0.6
Three-putts per round

87%
Putts made within 10 feet of the hole

6.9
One-putts per round

2'5"
Proximity to hole following first putt

Average numbers for 2006 PGA Tour. Stats courtesy of ShotLink.

SETUP AND STROKE BASICS

How to grip your putter, how to aim it and how to swing it to turn knee-knockers and lags into tap-ins

EYES
Your eyes should be directly over your line of putt.

FOREARMS
Your forearms should be level with each other. From this angle, your right forearm correctly hides your left forearm.

BALL
Your ball should be positioned so that it's even with the left side of your chest.

INSTRUCTION

How to Nail Your Alignment

This two-part check gives you a solid stance

Check 1: Forearms

Your forearms should be level with each other at address. There are two ways to check this. If there's someone else on the putting green, have him stand behind you along the line of your putt at address and look at your forearms. Your right forearm should hide your left forearm. If you're alone, take your address position and look down at your forearms—if they're level with one another, you're good to go.

Check 2: Eyes

At address, your eyes should be directly over your ball and your line of putt. This is crucial—even if your forearms are correct, if your eyes are too far outside the ball or too far inside the ball, a consistent path will be almost impossible. If you're not sure whether your eyes are over the line at address, check their position by dropping a ball from the bridge of your nose. If your eyes are too far forward, the ball will land outside your ball on the ground. If your eyes are too far inside the line of your putt, the dropped ball will land inside the ball on the ground.
—Tom Patri

NO! Your arms are uneven and closed to the line of the putt.

NO! Your arms are uneven and open to the line of the putt.

NO! Your eyes are too far inside the line of putt.

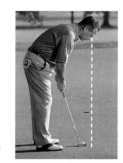

NO! Your eyes are too far outside the line of the putt.

How to be Automatic from Mid-Range

These drills will help you make the ones you should

1. Go on a bender

The fault it fixes: Breaking putts give you fits.

How to do it: Commit yourself to aiming at a spot other than the hole on short benders. Place a tee on the edge of the hole at 5 o'clock (the far side of the hole is 12 o'clock) for right-to-left breakers , and 7 o'clock for left-to-right breakers. Try to putt around the tee so the break feeds the ball into the hole. This will force you to pick a spot outside the hole and putt directly at it.

On breaking putts, swinging toward the hole won't get it done.

2. Track 'em

The fault it fixes: You have no confidence in your stroke.

How to do it: Build confidence in your stroke before you head to the first tee by laying two clubs along the ground so they form a path that ends at the hole, then putt five-footers between the shafts. Seeing the ball drop into the cup, even if it kisses off some steel, will get your mind thinking that you can make everything you look at.

3. Adjust for slope

The fault it fixes: You roll downhill putts way past the roll and come up short when putting uphill.

How to do it: See below to roll it right.

UPHILL
Press a tee under the lip of the hole on the uphill side, then hit your putts firmly enough so they strike the tee before dropping in.

DOWNHILL
Press a tee under the lip on the downhill side of the cup, leaving most of it exposed. Try to make putts without hitting the tee.

Line on ball parallel to clubface

4. Line up

The fault it fixes: You push or pull putts.

How to do it: Follow the steps below to learn how to strike the ball with a square putterface.

Step 1
Mark a straight line from the number on the ball through the center of the brand name as shown.

Step 2
Position the line you drew on the ball perpendicular to the target line.

Step 3
At address, set your putterface parallel to the line you drew on the ball.

Step 4
Strive to line up your putterface and the line you drew on the ball on your forward stroke. If you see the logo rolling tightly end over end, you'll know the putter was square. If the logo looks wobbly, keep practicing.
—Chuck Winstead

How to Make a Money Stroke

One thin dime can change you from a hitter to a stroker

Fault: You stab at the ball with your putter rather than making a smooth stroke, giving you zero speed control.

Fix: Place a dime on the back of your putter as shown and make your normal stroke. If you're stroking your putts using a pure pendulum motion, the dime will stay on the putter, no matter how far back and through you take it. If you're stabbing the ball, however, the dime will slide off the back of your club as soon as you transition from your backstroke to your forward stroke. You may not be able to tell if you're decelerating, but a dime will pick it up instantly.

—Dr. Jim Suttie

Deceleration will knock the dime off your putter here... ...while a smooth pendulum stroke will make sure it's on here.

Add Smooth to Your Stroke

Swing from low to high to generate a purer roll

To generate true roll with minimal bouncing or skidding, you must swing the putter slightly upward through impact. Set most of your weight over your right foot and you'll discover that your putter will naturally—and correctly—swing back lower and finish higher. If you address the ball with most of your weight over your left foot, you'll make a descending strike that presses the ball into the turf and causes it to hop off line.

—Eddie Merrins

How to Make a Model Stroke

The secret is in the design of your putter

The myth
Depending on your preference, swing your putterhead straight-back-and-through or on a slight arc.

The truth
The design of your putter— not your preferred putting style— determines the type of path you should trace. Toe-weighted putters are engineered to open and close during your stroke and travel on an arc, and face-balanced models (ones that feature a centered shaft connection or a double-bend shaft) are engineered to remain square and travel on a straight line.

What to do
Match your stroke to your putter, or buy a model that's designed to complement your putting style.

If your putter is face-balanced...
Take it back and through on a straight line keeping the face square all the way.

Allow your arms to hang directly underneath your shoulders.

Bend from your hips more to get your eyes over the target line.

Play the ball slightly forward of center with the putterhead directly below your nose.

Face-balanced stroke
Move the putter straight back and through by rocking your shoulders like a teeter-totter. To ingrain the feel of this stroke, place a club across your chest as shown and secure it underneath your armpits. Hit some putts by pointing the triangle formed by the club and your arms away from the target and then to the target.

If your putter is toe-weighted...
Take it away to the inside of your target line, return it square and finish back on the inside.

Play the ball off your left armpit.

Stand erect, with your eyes inside the target line.

Position your hands in front of your shoulder line.

Toe-weighted stroke
Since your hands are outside your arms, you'll naturally move the putter to the inside. The key is to maintain a free-flowing motion so you don't disturb the integrity of the arc. Practice putting with your left arm only to develop a free-swinging motion. Think of how a gate swings open and shut on its hinges—that's the feeling you're after.
—Mike Adams

Get Your Putts on the Right Track

Use a CD to make sure your eyes are over the ball

Use an old CD to see where your eyes sit at address. Eyes inside or outside the ball decrease the likelihood of hitting the putt on your intended line.

Fault: You consistently pull or push putts because your eyes are either too far inside the ball at address (causing a push) or too far outside the ball at address (causing a pull).

Fix: Position a ball in the little hole in the middle of an old music CD, shiny side up. Address the ball as if you were going to putt it and check where your eyes reflect on the CD. If your eyes are inside the ball, bend slightly forward from your hips until they move over the middle of the CD. If your eyes are outside the ball, bend slightly back from your hips. Positioning your eyes over the ball gives you the best view of the line and stops pull and push strokes in their tracks.
—Scott Sackett

Is Your Putter Ruining Your Stroke?

If the shaft is too long or short for you, the answer is yes

Your putter is too short...

If you have zero elbow bend

When the handle is so low that your have to straighten your arms to take your grip, it forces you to tip your shoulders up and down to make your stroke. You'll have distance-control problems because you'll make contact with a different amount of loft on every stroke.

Your putter is too long...

If your arms are jammed into your sides at address

When you grip an overly long putter, you're forced to bend your elbows too much, and when you swing your putter your body will get in the way. Choking down will only alter your putter's swingweight and send your tempo out of whack.

Your putter is just right...

If your arms hang under your shoulders when you grip the top of the handle

Look for elbows just under your rib cage with a slight amount of flex, which allows your arms and shoulders to swing the putter under your body without excess wrist and head motion.
—Todd Sones

Check the Hosel
Make sure it benefits your stroke

If you often pull putts, you'll fare better with a flare-tip hosel design, which holds off the rotation of the face. If you push putts, try a center-shafted putter (such as the straight-in), which gives you more direct control of the putterface.

If your stroke is straight-back-and-straight through, you'll putt more consistently with a face-balanced putter. Most face-balanced putters come with a double-bend shaft. On the other hand, if you're more of a "Crenshaw" putter, and like to gently roll the putter on an "inside-to-square-to-inside" stroke, you'll be better off with a hosel/shaft attachment that favors the heel.

Plumber-neck hosels really help you see if your putter is aligned at the target. But they also impact your hand position. If you strive to keep your hands ahead of the putter at impact, which many good putters do, an offset design like a plumber-neck will help.

Straight-in

Slant-neck

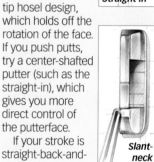
Flare-tip

Double-bend

Plumber-neck

Make Yours an Alternative Grip

Grips that buck tradition can help solve many putting problems

IF MOST OF YOUR MISSED PUTTS END UP LEFT OF THE HOLE...

Try a saw grip

This putting grip guides your hands and arms like you're sawing wood. If you recall the last time you cut wood, your hands and arms move along the same line as the cut. Similarly, a saw putting stroke swings your putter straight back and forth along your intended target line. There's no rotation so the putterface remains square and your tendency to pull putts disappears.

There are four main variations of the saw grip.

Perpendicular saw
Thumb and last three fingers of the right hand positioned forward of the shaft.

TRY IT If you can't stop releasing your forearms and closing the putterface.

Claw saw
Right hand folded around the grip and right hand and arm in line with the shaft.

TRY IT If your putterface rotates left after impact. The claw saw will keep your putter moving squarely down the line.

Parallel saw
Looks and feels like the standard right-hand position used for sawing wood.

TRY IT If your putter path heads left in your follow-through. This saw grip will smooth your stroke and harness right-hand power.

Vertical saw
Last three fingers of the right hand placed behind but in line with shaft.

TRY IT If you cut putts and often miss to the right. This grip keeps your putter square and on-line if your left wrist breaks down.
—Dave Pelz

With a regular right-hand-low grip [above], your shoulders tilt at address. A left-hand-low grip levels them out.

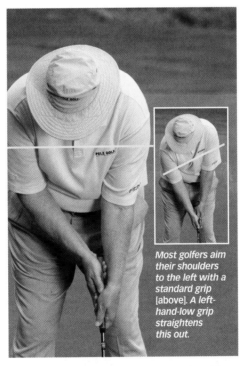

Most golfers aim their shoulders to the left with a standard grip [above]. A left-hand-low grip straightens this out.

IF YOU HAVE DIFFICULTY CONTROLLING THE SPEED OF YOUR PUTTS...

Go left hand low

Gripping your putter with your right hand lower than your left seems to make sense because that's how you hold all of your other clubs. With your putter, however, a right-hand-low grip tends to set your shoulder alignment left and tilt your right shoulder down.

A left-hand-low grip promotes good shoulder alignment and an on-line putter path. It also places your right hand in a submissive position behind your left wrist and forearm—this all but eliminates wrist hinge in your follow-through, even if you push too hard with your right hand. Your ability to control speed and distance will improve noticeably.
—Dave Pelz

Face First

A major key to consistently putting the ball the correct distance is making consistent contact in the center of your putterface. Contact out toward the toe or heel results in far less energy transfer, which also explains why you roll your ball way past the hole on one putt and then roll it way short the next, even with the same stroke.

To improve your contact consistency, wrap two rubber bands around the left and right sides of your putter's sweet spot. Practicing with the bands on your putter instantly tells you when you fail to stroke the ball in the center of your face. You'll feel a "thud" rather than a "click," meaning you missed the center and hit one of the bands. For feel putters, it's either centered contact or bust.
—Lynn Marriott

Hitting the ball on the sweet spot is the key to distance control.

JUDGE LINE, SPEED & BREAK

The best stroke in the world won't get the ball in the hole unless you know how the putt will react to the green once it gets rolling. Try these time-honored techniques for picking the right line.

How to Stay on Your Line

A five-step plan to get your putts tracking from the start

It's critical to build a setup that gives you the best chance to get your ball rolling in the right direction, because a ball that starts off line stays off line. Here's a five-step plan to correctly position your body and putter on the line you've chosen.
—Donald Crawley

Step 1:
Find your line
On the practice green, stand behind your ball and imagine how it will roll. Run a raised string along the starting point of the line and burn the image of what your starting line looks like into your brain. This physical representation of your putt line will give you an idea of what a straight line actually looks like.

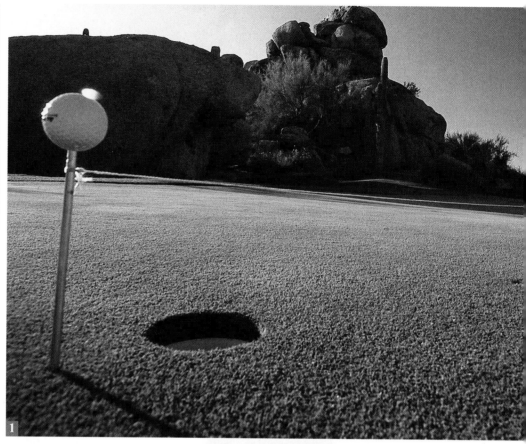

Step 2:
Align your ball
Draw a straight line across the logo on your ball. Use this mark to align your ball along the intended line of the putt by placing it underneath and parallel to the static line. Now you have a reference point to get your putterface pointed in the right direction.

Step 3:
Aim your putter
Remove the string and sole your putterhead on the ground. Align the face so that the top edge makes a perpendicular angle with the mark on your ball. This will ensure that your putter starts the ball on the correct line after contact, as long as you don't dramatically open or close the face during your stroke.

Step 4:
Set your eyes
Set your eyes over the ball and parallel to your intended line. If you set your eyes to the inside of the ball your stroke will have a tendency to move inside and push your putts; set your eyes outside and you'll likely pull your putts. Either way, you'll miss the putt.

A physical representation of your line can be very helpful.

5

Step 5:
Align your body
Allow your arms to hang straight down from your shoulders, and then place your hands on the grip. Loose, free-hanging arms are needed to create the tension-free stroke that you need to be a consistent putter.

Be a Green-Reading Detective

All the clues to the break are out in the open

While a good course designer will do his best to challenge your green-reading abilities, he'll also leave obvious clues about how the ball will roll on different areas of the green. If you know what to look for, you'll know the general slope of the green even before you get behind your ball. —Todd Sones

Clue 1

PUTTS BREAK AWAY FROM HILLS
Don't forget the obvious. Putts will break away from greenside bumps, hills and rises, especially if they're close to the line of your putt.

Clue 2

PUTTS BREAK AWAY FROM THE CLUBHOUSE
While not always true, clubhouses are normally built on the highest point on the course. Look for home, and you'll get a good idea of the general lay of the land— information that can come in handy when you can't tell exactly which way a putt falls.

Clue 3

PUTTS BREAK TOWARD WATER
For obvious drainage reasons, greens will slope toward the nearest body of water. On oceanside courses, don't underestimate the natural roll of terrain toward the sea—putts break especially hard toward the agua here.

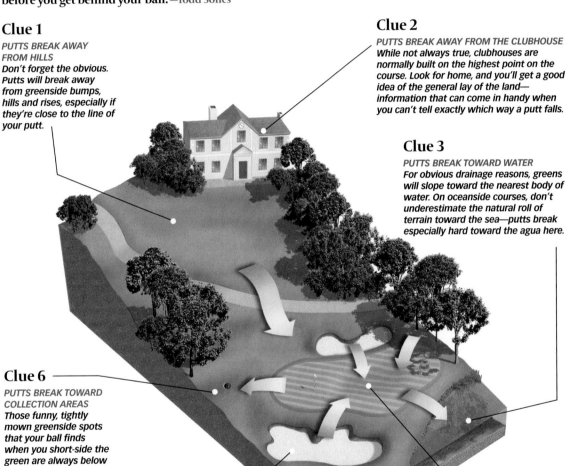

Clue 6

PUTTS BREAK TOWARD COLLECTION AREAS
Those funny, tightly mown greenside spots that your ball finds when you short-side the green are always below the level of the putting surface, and they usually house a drain at the lowest point. If you're putting near one of these collection areas, the break will favor that direction.

Clue 5

PUTTS BREAK AWAY FROM BUNKERS
The last thing a course designer—and especially the superintendent— wants is water draining into a bunker. More often than not, the green slopes away from the sand to avoid extra bunker maintenance.

Clue 4

PUTTS BREAK TOWARD THE SUN
The grass on the green grows all day long, following the path of the sun. In the late afternoon, when the blades are at their longest, greens feature a serious grain toward the setting sun. Your putts will break with the grain. This clue is especially important when playing on long-blade Bermuda grass.

"On the practice green, walk off 10 paces and make a mental note of the stroke it takes to roll putts that distance. Use that as a guide for all putts during your round."
—Donald Crawley

THE NEW WAYS TO PUTT

Tried-and-true techniques never go out of style— unless the ball isn't going into the hole. Then it's time to try something new.

How to Roll With the Right Speed

This drill will give you the right pace for short putts

Fault: You leave short putts short, or they lose their line due to a lack of speed

Fix: Secure a scorecard pencil between two sets of tees in front of the hole as shown at right. Putt a few balls from anywhere from three to five feet from the hole. The idea is to hit these putts with enough force that the ball pops over the pencil and then into the hole. You'll quickly learn that to sink your putts with the proper amount of speed; you can't baby the ball to the cup, nor can you rocket it because too much speed will pop the ball over both the pencil and the hole.

Once you get to the point where you can consistently pop eight out of 10 putts over the pencil and into the hole, remove the pencil and try to sink your putts with the same velocity through the two tees—these putts should always hit somewhere on the back of the cup. Then remove the tees and work on maintaining the same speed and line.
—Dr. Gary Wiren

The speed that will pop the ball over a pencil and into the cup is perfect for short putts.

INSTRUCTION

Be Firm With Downhillers

Forget the sweet spot—off-center impact keeps you from jabbing at nasty sliders

The situation
You're facing a slick, downhill breaker. The tendency under these circumstances is to make a super-short, jabby stroke.

The solution
You have to impart enough energy into the ball to get it started, but if you quit on the stroke there's a good chance the ball will skip off line. Think back to how dead the impact felt the last time you mistakenly struck a putt off-center toward the toe—and how far short of the hole you ended up. That's your key.

Why it works
By making contact toward the toe, you spill energy instead of transferring it. The ball will start on the line you selected, but only the slope and slickness of the green will act to keep it in motion. Through friction and gravity, the ball tends to die—safely in or near the hole.

How to toe it
Set up to deaden your impact

1. Address this putt so the toe of your putter is aligned with the outside third of the ball [photo above].

2. Rehearse a short, slow backswing and a deliberate forward swing. Hold the putter firmly enough to prevent your "toe hit" from opening up the blade.

3. Step up to the ball and make the same stroke. You'll create "dead" impact to offset the slick conditions.
—**Eden Foster**

INSTRUCTION

How to Putt Under Pressure
Use this drill to turn knee-knockers into kick-ins

On short pressure-packed putts, it's vital to keep your head and body still. If you lift your head to watch the ball you'll pull your shoulders and the putterhead off line, causing the putt to miss to the left. To stay still, try pinching your knees inward. As you make your stroke, let your ears be your eyes: Listen for the ball to hit the bottom of the hole—that means no peeking!
—**Mark Wood**

Cave in your knees, not in to pressure.

A Better Way to Putt

After analyzing nearly 3,000 putts, our research reveals there's a better way to get the ball into the hole

The conventional wisdom

You should look at the ball for the duration of your putting stroke, and keep your eyes on that spot until well after the ball has been struck.

The unconventional theory

You should look at the hole–not the ball–from the moment you set the club behind the ball until you complete your putting stroke.

The Study

40 players ranging in handicap from eight to 36. They were divided into two 20-person groups, with each group balanced in terms of handicap, age and gender. One was the experimental group. The other was the control group. This control group used the conventional method of looking at the ball while putting throughout the test.

The Experiment

Using the conventional method of looking at the ball, both groups putted nine balls to holes ranging from three feet to 43 feet away. The results were statistically equal.

Next, the control group putted one ball to each of nine targets in random order. The experimental group did the same but with one huge change: They were instructed to go through their normal pre-putt routine, but rather than looking at the ball as they made their stroke, they were told to look at the hole.

Then we compared the two groups. How did looking at the hole measure up? The results will surprise you.

The New Way to Putt

1 Address the ball and place your putter behind it.

2 Start looking at the hole, and don't look back at the ball. (We promise it's still there.)

3 Hit your putt, and keep looking at the hole until you complete your stroke.

Rather than looking at the ball as they made their stroke (left), the subjects were told to look at the hole the entire time (right).

The Shocking Results!

● **Long putts end up significantly closer to the hole when you look at the hole while making your stroke**. On average, after all was said and done, on putts between 28 feet and 43 feet in length, the experimental group (those who looked at the hole) had slightly less than 28 inches remaining to the hole.

By comparison, on the same long putts, the control group (those who looked at the ball) left themselves nearly 37 inches remaining to the hole. That means the experimental group was 24 percent closer, nine inches that could be the difference between a two-putt and a three-putt.

● **Looking at the hole may be more effective on short putts, too.** On putts between three feet and eight feet, the experimental group left an average of just under nine inches to the hole. On the same putts, the control group ended up with leaves that averaged 12.5 inches. Strictly speaking, that's not statistically significant, but those inches might be the difference between a routine tap-in and the occasional short miss.

"On average, after all was said and done, on putts between 28 feet and 43 feet in length, the experimental group (those who looked at the hole) had slightly less than 28 inches remaining to the hole."
—Eric Alpenfels

MORE RESULTS:
Two other facts of note from our research: From 13 to 23 feet, both methods produced similar results. Neither method produced more holed putts from any distance.

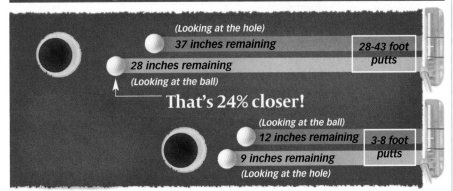

Putts end up closer when you look at the hole

(Looking at the hole)
37 inches remaining

28 inches remaining
(Looking at the ball)

28-43 foot putts

That's 24% closer!

(Looking at the ball)
12 inches remaining

9 inches remaining
(Looking at the hole)

3-8 foot putts

Any golfer who's had an important putt burn the lip of the hole knows every inch is precious on the green. This graph clearly shows that looking at the hole, not the ball, will pay off dramatically.

Why it works

There are three main reasons why the new method improves on your old one:

1 You're using both eyes to to see your target, giving you highly accurate depth perception.

2 Maybe it was a fear of whiffing the putt, but testers who looked at the hole maintained their posture like statues.

3 Testers who looked at the hole didn't decelerate through the ball. In other words, they established natural speed control.
—Eric Alpenfels

Are You a Candidate?

Should you look at the hole instead of the ball when you putt?

Take this test and find out:

Q: Do you typically three-putt more than twice per round?
Yes ❏   No ❏

Q: Do you consistently leave yourself a putt of more than five feet after hitting a 25-footer?
Yes ❏   No ❏

Q: Do you take longer than two seconds to pull the trigger after your last look at the hole?
Yes ❏   No ❏

Q: Do you second-guess yourself after you've addressed the ball more than twice per round?
Yes ❏   No ❏

Q: Do you find it hard to strike putts aggressively and avoid decelerating?
Yes ❏   No ❏

Score: *If you answered yes this many times...*

0: We still need a partner for the member-guest, but you're probably too busy playing in the U.S. Open.

1-2: You might think it sounds quirky, but it could be all that's standing between you and breaking your next scoring barrier.

3 or more: You've got nothing to lose.

You're going to find trouble every time you play. The trick isn't avoiding it—it's learning to get out of it.

SECTION 9

TROUBLE SHOTS

Even the best-made plans sometimes go haywire. Here's how to get out of any predicament on the course.

Face facts: you'll never play a round when you hit every shot off tightly mown grass with a level lie. Bad shots happen, and even good ones end up in trouble via bad bounces, strange kicks and other "rub of the green" effects that defy explanation but nonetheless are a very real part of the game.

A trouble situation is any one that prohibits you from making your regular swing. Most often it takes the form of an obstacle between you and your target. Other times it's the lie itself, like when your ball comes to rest in ankle-deep rough or in a sand-filled divot. When you think of how many times you alter your technique to accommodate anything but a perfect lie, you realize just how often trouble shots pop up during the normal course of play.

Point is, finding trouble is something every golfer does. The trick is getting out of it. It's bad enough to find trouble, let alone use two or three swings to get back on the fairway or green. Using this section to tackle every possible trouble situation is difficult—there are far too many. Instead, the Top 100 Teachers describe how to overcome the most common forms. Learn and perfect these escapes and you'll be sitting pretty—even when your ball isn't.

5 THINGS YOU'LL LEARN IN THIS SECTION

- How to keep trouble shots to a minimum
- How to hit over, under and around trees that block the path to your target
- How to escape rough with maximum power
- Easy ways to get back into play when your stance and swing are obstructed
- How to hit chips from difficult situations around the green with unusual swings

How to Avoid Trouble at the Beginning

I'm sick of getting into trouble on the first three holes or so. Is there a way to get my rounds off to better starts?

"If you're tired of relying on trouble shots while your game is still sputtering out of the blocks, try this trick one of my Tour students uses. Instead of ending your pre-round warm-up on the practice putting green, end it on the driving range. To finish up your prep, hit the shots you'll need on the first, second and third holes, from the drive to the approach shot. Hit in reverse order (3rd, 2nd, 1st) so that the first hole is fresh in your mind when you head to the tee. Visualize each fairway, and then go through your normal pre-shot routine (picking out a target, visualizing the shot shape) before hitting each shot. This routine will put you in full scoring mode from the beginning and place less pressure on your trouble game."
—**Pat Goss**

HOW TO GET OUT OF TROUBLE

Each situation is unique. The key is to get creative and stay confident.

INSTRUCTION

How to Hit Out of Trees

Choke down to keep it low

The situation

You've missed the fairway, and though your lie is good and you're only 100 yards from the green, a low-hanging branch prevents you from playing a wedge shot.

The strategy

Step 1: Stay aggressive—never let a tree or its limbs come between you and a chance for birdie.
Step 2: Determine which is the highest-lofted club in your bag that will keep the ball under the branch.
Step 3: Mix and match your grip (how much you choke down on the handle) and backswing length to produce the appropriate distance.

How to do it

For the shot depicted here, a 6-iron is the highest loft that will keep the ball under the limb. Let's say you normally hit a 6-iron 160 yards. Here's the trick to hitting it the 100 yards you need.
—Dr. Gary Wiren

KEY MOVE
This technique only works if you swing to a full finish. The ball will fly low enough to avoid the trouble and travel far enough to stop safely on the green.

160 yds
Take your normal grip on the end of the handle.

150 yds
Now choke down to the middle of the grip. This takes 10 yards off the shot.

140 yds
If you choke all the way down to the bottom, that subtracts 10 more yards.

Make a Back-Handed Escape

Here's what to do when an obstacle interferes with your stance

Choose one of your wedges—these have the largest faces and you'll benefit from a broader hitting area since you won't be looking at the ball during contact.

Step 1
Turn your back to the target, stand about a half-foot to the right of the ball and grip your wedge in the middle of the handle. Flip your club around so that the face points at your target with the club resting on its toe.

Step 2
Cock your club up by bending your right elbow (keep your upper arm still). Add just a touch of wrist hinge.

Step 3
Straighten your arm and slap your clubhead into the back of the ball.

This is a trick shot that's actually very easy to pull off with a little practice. Make sure you accelerate all the way to the ball so the club doesn't flip past your hands and hit the ball thin.
—Tom F. Stickney II

OPTION-MINDED
Mixing and matching the three choke distances with the three different backswing lengths allows you to produce seven distances with each one of your irons.

140 yds
With a full swing you'll still produce 140 yards— that's too much.

120 yds
Shorten your backswing by 10 inches (hands chest high) to hit it 20 yards less.

100 yds
Shorten your backswing another 10 inches (hands at hip height) to take off another 20 yards.

INSTRUCTION

Escape Rough With Your Worst Swing

Fix your slice for straighter drives, but keep it in your pocket to save par from nasty lies

The situation

On the tee, you hoist your driver like you're trying to squish a bug on a 10-foot ceiling. On the way back down, you make a severe cut and leave a sizable divot on the tee box. There's no "around" to your swing—it's all up-and-down. The result: a 165-yard slice that lands in a patch of nasty, thick rough.

The silver lining

You're now faced with 200+ yards to the green. You need some distance on your second shot so you can play your third shot close to the pin. The good news: with a mid-iron and that ugly, steep, cut swing you made on the tee, you'll be in business.

The steep cut swing associated with slicing limits contact with the grass for extra-long escapes from the rough.

How to slice it from the rough

1 The slice swing starts by taking the club up vertically so that your hands are way above your shoulders.

2 From the top, come down steeply and allow your clubhead to move outside your hands.

3 Swing to the left of the target to complete the over-the-top move and escape the rough with power.

Why it works

The major problem with rough is that it gets between your ball and the clubface. You'll always suffer a loss of distance as a result. Plus, the long grass tends to grab the hosel through impact and close the face, making it impossible to control the ball.

A steep cut swing solves both of these problems. With your club approaching the ball on a steeper angle of attack, there's less contact time between the clubface and the grass, so your shots will fly nearly full distance. And since your clubface is open (a natural byproduct of a cut path), the shutdown from the grass will make everything flush at contact.

—Eden Foster

Hosel It From Deep Grass

The part of the club that causes shanks can help you make a great escape from deep lies

Just getting the clubface on the ball in deep rough (never mind moving it forward) can be tough. But here's how to use the whole clubhead—including the hosel—to muscle the ball out of the junk.

Step 1
Stiffen the clubshaft
Choke down about an inch or so on the handle of your sand wedge or pitching wedge. This will help stiffen the shaft (make it stronger) and allow the clubhead to cut through the grass more effectively at impact.

Step 2
Get more mass behind the ball
Sole your club with the face slightly closed and the ball in the "V" formed by the clubface and the hosel. This will get more of the clubhead's weight (most of it is in the hosel) behind the ball at impact, and the opposing clubface and hosel angles will keep your ball on target.

Step 3
Lean the handle forward
Set up with the ball off the inside of your right heel and lean the shaft forward by moving your hands toward the target. This promotes a steeper swing angle, which allows the clubhead to pass through as little grass as possible.

Step 4
Swing up and down sharply
Use extra wrist hinge and keep your follow-through to a minimum, as you would for a buried lie in a bunker. You almost want to feel as though you're leaving the clubhead in the grass.
—**Patti McGowan**

Tilt the club on its toe.

Make a level strike and allow for plenty of roll.

Beat the Collar

Hit it thin when you're against it

The situation
The ball is against the collar of the green—the long grass behind the ball makes clean contact almost impossible.

The play
Hit a "bellied wedge," striking the center of the ball (the part that lies above the collar grass) with the leading edge of your sand wedge.

How to do it
At address, push the shaft away from you so that the leading edge lines up diagonally across the ball. This little trick ensures that at least some part of the club's leading edge will strike the ball's equator. Take a couple of practice swings, keeping the clubhead fairly level. Expect the shot to come out hot with no backspin.
—**Bill Moretti**

Working on your game won't stop you from never hitting a bad shot again, but it will stop you from hitting the same bad shot twice during play.

SECTION 10

FLAWS AND FIXES

How to make sure you don't make the same mistake twice when bad habits creep into your swing

I t doesn't matter who you are, how long you've been playing or how low your handicap is—you're going to hit bad shots in every round. The key to turning poor rounds into good ones (and good ones into great ones) is to not hit the same bad shot more than once. Since bad shots always come in groups, you can save loads of strokes by stopping a negative trend before it builds momentum.

Owning the ability to quick-fix your game on the course is the hallmark of any great player. Granted, you need practice to completely eradicate flaws in your technique, but Band Aid fixes can and do work, or at the very least can stop the bleeding during your bad rounds.

In this section, the Top 100 Teachers address the most common swing flaws. Their fixes are simple—you can use them during play or as the foundation for a practice session dedicated to completely working out your kinks. That's the way to make sure your fixes stick. The flaws addressed on the following pages are only the tip of the fault iceberg. Luckily, fixing these takes care of much of the rest. In fact, eliminating just half of these disaster shots will make your next round a nice, low number.

5 THINGS YOU'LL LEARN IN THIS SECTION

- How to stop short-game errors like hitting your iron shots thin and hitting your chip shots fat
- How to get a feel for distance on less-than-full wedges
- Self-diagnose your bunker problems
- How to swing on plane more consistently and three ways to fix your slice—and one to fix your hook
- How to stop topping your drives and hit for more power off the tee

YOUR GAME

What Makes Your Shots Curve?

There are nine different ways to approach a golf ball, which result in nine possible ball flights. Here are the path/face combinations that cause them. Look for yours to discover exactly what you should be working on.

1 Straight: Swing path along target line, clubface square

2 Hook: Path along line, face closed

3 Slice: Path along line, face open

4 Pull: Path out-to-in, face square to path

5 Pull-hook: Path out-to-in, face closed to path

6 Pull-slice: Path out-to-in, face open to path

7 Push: Path in-to-out, face square to path

8 Push-hook: Path in-to-out, face closed to path

9 Push-slice: Path in-to-out, face open to path

A fade is a controlled pull-slice; a draw a controlled push-hook.

Stop Topping Your Tee Shots

Use these three fixes to turn your dribblers into drives

Cause

There's more than one way to top a drive. The big three are:

1. Dropkick

You swing on a steep, inside-out plane and the sole of the club bounces off the ground well behind the ball.

2. Near whiff

You lift up at impact, and the sole of your driver contacts the top of the ball in a "near-miss" attempt. The ball barely topples forward off the tee.

3. Thin skim

You swing on a steep, outside-in plane, resulting in a glancing blow off the top of the ball that sends it scurrying along the ground.

Fix 1: Dropkick
Your swing is steep and too inside-out

An inside-out swing plane in and of itself can be a good thing. It promotes a draw, which will help you add distance. It's when you overdo it that you create the dropkick. On your downswing, strive to contact the inside lower quadrant of the ball, but rotate your hands so that the club exits the hitting area on a line that parallels your target line. Try to "throw" the clubhead at your target.

Swing your club down the target line after impact.

WRONG!

Don't swing too far from the inside.

Fix 2: Near whiff
You raise up at impact

To ensure that you stay down and through the ball, keep your knees flexed—but relaxed—throughout your swing, and keep your right heel on the ground for as long as possible. Also, resist the urge to "slap" at the ball, and instead focus on swinging through it, with your right shoulder turning under your chin through the hitting area. You don't need to help the ball into the air—the club will do that for you.

Fix 3: Thin skim
Your swing is steep and too outside-in

To stop your right shoulder from pulling your clubhead across the line, address the ball with your right shoulder lower than your left, and bend your right elbow so that it sits closer to your torso than your left. These fixes will help you make the correct turn and will keep your shoulder movement in check, helping your club to remain on plane.

—**Laird Small**

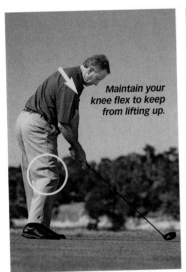

Maintain your knee flex to keep from lifting up.

Set your right shoulder low to help keep your club on plane.

WRONG!

Don't raise up or straighten your right knee.

WRONG!

Don't pull your shoulders across the ball.

Why Can't I Escape the Sand?

Here are four common causes for bunker blues—and four easy ways to make a great escape

1 AM I HITTING TOO FAR BEHIND THE BALL?
Hitting four, five or six inches behind the ball is too far. The club should enter the sand about two inches behind for greenside shots.

TEST
Draw a line in the sand up to your ball, perpendicular to the target. Measure where your divot starts. More than 3 inches behind is too far.

FIX No. 1
Visualize your ball resting on the center of a dollar bill. When you swing, your club should enter the back of the dollar and exit the front, creating a bill-shaped divot.

NO? YES!

2 AM I FAILING TO SHIFT MY WEIGHT?
Swinging just with your arms, and not shifting your weight, decelerates the club. The ugly outcome: bladed shots.

TEST
Swing! Now check your feet. Is your leading foot flat in the finish position? That means you're not pivoting your weight toward the target.

FIX No. 2
Take practice swings until you can splash sand onto the green. That forces you to make an aggressive, full-body swing.

NO? YES!

3 AM I TOO HANDSY?
In a greenside bunker, it's tempting to flip your wrist instead of making a full turn. But you'll lose the "pop" needed to escape.

TEST
If most of your shots barely sneak over the lip, you're all hands.

FIX No. 3
Be a one-armed bunker bandit! To promote a full turn back and through, choke down to the middle of the grip with your right hand and hit one-armed shots.

—**Rick Grayson**

Stop Slicing

Try these three drills to eliminate your banana ball for good

Drill 1:
Fix your plane

Grip a mid-iron in just your left hand and, with your right hand, hold a second mid-iron by its hosel. Take your normal address and position the grip of the club in your right hand about six inches behind the clubhead of the one in your left *[photo, far right]*. Swing both clubs slowly to the top, doing your best to keep them exactly six inches apart.

If both of the shafts feel light in your hands and are still parallel (use a mirror or ask a friend to watch you), you found the correct plane—ingrain that feel.

Why it works

If you make the common mistake of swinging too much around your back (below the correct plane) or over your head (above the correct plane) rather than around your shoulders, gravity will cause one or both clubs to feel heavy.
—**Brad Redding**

You're on plane if both clubs are parallel and feel light in your hands.

This drill will get you on plane in seconds.

Drill 2:
Hit a homerun

(1) Address a ball in the middle of your stance, then leaving your right foot in place move your left foot back until your feet touch, **(2)** swing to the top and on the way down move your left foot back to its original position, and **(3)** make contact with both feet on the ground.

Why it works

This baseball-type swing forces you to begin your downswing with your lower body, which sets up an inside-out sequence (legs, shoulders, arms, hands and clubhead).
—**Darrell Kestner**

Drill 3:
Tell time

Save long-term swing fixes for the practice range and concentrate on this emergency cure. As you swing through impact, make a conscious effort to square up your clubface. If you're wearing a watch on your left wrist, try to allow an imaginary person standing behind you to see what time it is immediately following impact.

Why it works
It's a good trigger to remind you to rotate your forearms through the hitting area to prevent leaving the face open. Aim 10 yards right of your target in case the ball hooks a little.

After your round, forget this quick fix and try to determine the real cause of your slice. Most likely it's an outside-in downswing path. That requires more than a Band-Aid. But the watch trick works and can definitely help you turn a bad driving day into a decent scoring day.
—**Tom F. Stickney II**

QUICK TIP
If you still slice no matter what you do, try an offset driver. This design gives you more time to square the face.

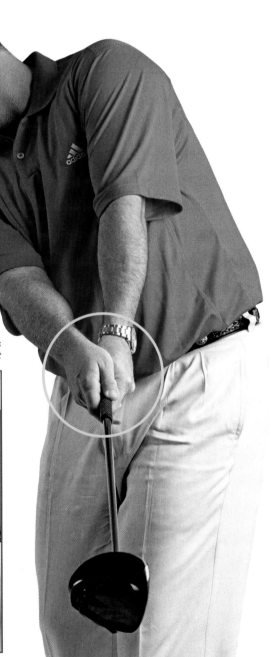

Rotate your forearms through impact

When a person behind you can tell the time on your watch, you've properly squared your clubface.

Stop Hooking the Ball
Think like the Karate Kid to chop this ugly shot

Cause
At impact, your clubface points to the left of both your target and your swing path.

Fix
Imagine you're making a karate chop at a board with the side, or heel, of your left hand on your downswing. This is the swing thought that helped Billy Casper get his hook under control. By leading with the side of your left hand, you delay the rotation of your forearms just enough to prevent the toe of the club from passing the heel too early. Thus, you can't turn the face over.

Why it works
Think of it this way: The back of your left hand mirrors the position of your clubface at impact, so if you can keep your knuckles pointing right of the target, your clubface will look that way, too. If the face looks right, there's no way you can curl the ball to the left.
—**Martin Hall**

Lead with the left side of your left hand—like you would when you make a karate chop—to reel in your hooks.

Stop Hitting Your Irons Fat

Strike the ball then take a walk

Cause
Your clubhead bottoms out behind the ball.

Fix
Try the "strike and stride." Take your normal setup with a 5-iron. Swing to the top, then step toward the target with your right foot as you start down [right]—a move made famous by Gary Player.

Why it works
As you step, your weight will shift onto your front foot. This moves the bottom of your swing arc forward so the clubhead strikes the ball before it hits the ground. The proof is in your divot, which will start on the target side of the ball.
—**Martin Hall**

Stranding weight on your right side places the bottom of your swing arc behind the ball.

Step forward on your downswing to move the bottom of your swing arc into the right place.

Imagining a football field will help your distance control.

INSTRUCTION

Stop Missing With Your Wedges

Here's how to hit it tight when you're left with an awkward distance to the hole

Set up open to your target line on wedge shots for a better turn.

Cause
You can't figure out how far to carry the ball and how far back to swing the club.

Fix
Visualize a football field on the fairway.

Why it works
By imagining lines every 10 yards from your ball to the hole, you'll focus on the exact distance to help you play the right shot. If the pin is in front, try to land your ball on the front fringe. If it's all the way back, you'll want to land it about halfway onto the green. Once you know how far you want to carry it, you'll control the distance with the length of your backswing.
—**Carol Preisinger**

DRILL

Stop Chunking Your Chips

If you're tired of sticking the club in the ground, then try practicing blindfolded

Cause
You dip your head down at impact.

Fix
Address the ball with your chipping club. Hold your chin as high as possible and extend your arms down to the ball.

● Wrap a handkerchief or T-shirt around your eyes. Once it's secure, re-position the club behind the ball and address the ball again. (You might have to peek to check.)

● Chip the ball. Keep your head and upper body high through the motion.

● Remove the blindfold. We'll bet you a five-spot that your ball ends up closer to the hole than your usual chip.

Why it works
The blindfold eliminates the "hit impulse" which causes you to focus too much on the ball and dip your chin in an effort to scoop it into the air.
—**Rick Barry**

THE TOP 100 TEACHERS IN AMERICA

A quick look at the nation's most exclusive—
and talented—team of teaching experts

MIKE ADAMS
Facility: Hamilton Farms G.C., Gladstone, N.J.
Website: www.mikeadamsgolf.com
Teaching since: 1977
Top 100 since: 1996
See Mike's tips on pages 43, 69 and 117

ROB AKINS
Facility: Ridgeway C.C., Germantown, Tenn.
Website: www.robakinsgolf.com
Teaching since: 1987
Top 100 since: 2001

ERIC ALPENFELS
Facility: The Pinehurst G.A., Pinehurst, N.C.
Website: www.pinehurst.com
Teaching since: 1984
Top 100 since: 2001
See Eric's tips on pages 26, 27, 68, 124 and 125

TODD ANDERSON
Facility: Sea Island Golf Learning Ctr., St. Simons Island, Ga.
Website: www.seaisland.com
Teaching since: 1984
Top 100 since: 2003
See Todd's tips on pages 70 and 71

ROBERT BAKER
Facility: Miami Beach G.C., Miami Beach, Fla.
Website: www.logicalgolf.com
Teaching since: 1989
Top 100 since: 1999
See Robert's tips on pages 41, 49, 58, 59, 72 and 73

RICK BARRY
Facility: Sea Pines Resort, Hilton Head Island, S.C.
Website: www.seapines.com
Teaching since: 1976
Top 100 since: 2005
See Rick's tips on page 139

MIKE BENDER
Facility: Mike Bender G.A. at Timacuan C.C., Lake Mary, Fla.
Website: www.mikebender.com
Teaching since: 1990
Top 100 since: 1996
See Mike's tips on pages 37 and 43

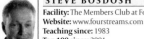

STEVE BOSDOSH
Facility: The Members Club at Four Streams
Website: www.fourstreams.com
Teaching since: 1983
Top 100 since: 2001
See Steve's tips on pages 25, 35, 88 and 105

MICHAEL BREED
Facility: Sunningdale C.C., Scarsdale, N.Y.
Website: None
Teaching since: 1986
Top 100 since: 2003
See Mike's tips on pages 24, 25, 54, 61, 65 and 81

BRAD BREWER
Facility: Brad Brewer G.A. at Shingle Creek, Orlando, Fla.
Website: www.bradbrewer.com
Teaching since: 1984
Top 100 since: 2007
See Brad's tips on page 31

HENRY BRUNTON
Facility: Henry Brunton Golf, Maple, Ontario
Website: www.henrybrunton.com
Teaching since: 1985
Top 100 since: 2005

ANNE CAIN
Facility: Anne Cain G.A. at Amelia Island G.C., Amelia Island, Fla.
Website: www.annecaingolf.com
Teaching since: 1995
Top 100 since: 2007
See Anne's tips on page 97

JASON CARBONE
Facility: Jim McLean G.S. at The Wigwam, Litchfield Park, Ariz.
Website: www.jimmclean.com/usa/wigwam
Teaching since: 1993
Top 100 since: 2007
See Jason's tips on pages 19 and 106

DONALD CRAWLEY
Facility: The Boulders Golf Academy, Carefree, Ariz.
Website: www.golfsimplified.com
Teaching since: 1974
Top 100 since: 1999
See Donald's tips on pages 91, 98, 120 and 121

JOHN DAHL
Facility: Oxbow C.C., Oxbow, N.D.
Website: www.oxbowcc.com
Teaching since: 1974
Top 100 since: 2003
See John's tips on pages 46 and 79

BILL DAVIS
Facility: Jupiter Hills Club, Tequesta, Fla.
Website: www.jupiterhillsclub.org
Teaching since: 1973
Top 100 since: 1996
See Bill's tips on page 101

MIKE DAVIS
Facility: Stallion Mountain C.C., Las Vegas, Nev.
Website: www.waltersgolf.com
Teaching since: 1970
Top 100 since: 2007
See Mike's tips on page 37

GLENN DECK
Facility: Pelican Hill G.A., Newport Coast, Calif.
Website: www.pelicanhill.com
Teaching since: 1983
Top 100 since: 2003
See Glenn's tips on page 93

DOM DiJULIA
Facility: Dom DiJulia G.S. at Jericho Nat'l G.C., New Hope, Pa.
Website: www.dijuliagolf.com
Teaching since: 1990
Top 100 since: 2007
See Dom's tips on page 45

JOHN ELLIOT, JR.
Facility: Golden Ocala Golf & Equestrian Club, Ocala, Fla.
Website: www.goldenocala.com
Teaching since: 1970
Top 100 since: 1996
See John's tips on pages 10, 36, 42, 45, 78 and 93

BILL FORREST
Facility: Troon Country Club, Scottsdale, Ariz.
Website: www.trooncc.com
Teaching since: 1978
Top 100 since: 2007
See Bill's tips on page 92

EDEN FOSTER
Facility: Maidstone Club, East Hampton, N.Y.
Website: www.maidstoneclub.com
Teaching since: 1988
Top 100 since: 2003
See Eden's tips on pages 91, 100, 108, 123 and 130

JANE FROST
Facility: Sandwich Hollows G.C., Sandwich, Mass.
Website: www.janefrostgolfschools.com
Teaching since: 1982
Top 100 since: 1996
See Jane's tips on page 15

BRYAN GATHRIGHT
Facility: Oak Hills C.C., San Antonio, Tex.
Website: www.oakhillscc.com
Teaching since: 1987
Top 100 since: 2001
See Bryan's tips on page 71

DAVID GLENZ
Facility: David Glenz G.A., Franklin, N.J.
Website: www.davidglenz.com
Teaching since: 1978
Top 100 since: 1996
See David's tips on page 20 and 47

CRAIG HARMON
Facility: Oak Hill C.C., Rochester, N.Y.
Website: www.oakhillcc.com
Teaching since: 1968
Top 100 since: 1996
See Craig's tips on page 19

SANDY LaBAUVE
Facility: Westin Kierland Resort and Spa, Scottsdale, Ariz.
Website: www.kierlandresort.com
Teaching since: 1984
Top 100 since: 1996
See Sandy's tips on page 59

PATRICK GOSS
Facility: Northwestern University, Evanston, Ill.
Website: www.northwestern.edu/athletics
Teaching since: 1993
Top 100 since: 2007
See Patrick's tips on page 126

SHAWN HUMPHRIES
Facility: Cowboys G.C., Grapevine, Tex.
Website: www.shawnhumphries.com
Teaching since: 1988
Top 100 since: 2005
See Shawn's tips on pages 21, 30, 31, 38, 39 and 80

ROD LIDENBERG
Facility: Prestwick G.C., Woodbury, Minn.
Website: www.pgamasterpro.com
Teaching since: 1972
Top 100 since: 2007
See Rod's tips on page 11

RICK GRAYSON
Facility: Connie Morris Golf Learning Center, Springfield, Mo.
Website: www.rickgraysongolf.com
Teaching since: 1976
Top 100 since: 1996
See Rick's tips on pages 61 and 135

DON HURTER
Facility: Castle Pines G.C., Castle Rock, Colo.
Website: None
Teaching since: 1987
Top 100 since: 2003
See Don's tips on pages 20 and 85

MIKE LOPUSZYNSKI
Facility: David Glenz G.A., Franklin, N.J.
Website: www.davidglenz.com
Teaching since: 1987
Top 100 since: 1996
See Mike's tips on page 7

FRED GRIFFIN
Facility: Grand Cypress Academy of Golf, Orlando, Fla.
Website: www.grandcypress.com
Teaching since: 1980
Top 100 since: 1996
See Fred's tips on pages 54 and 90

ED IBARGUEN
Facility: Duke University G.C., Durham, N.C.
Website: www.golf.duke.edu
Teaching since: 1979
Top 100 since: 2001
See Ed's tips on page 13

JACK LUMPKIN
Facility: Sea Island Golf Learning Ctr., St. Simons Island, Ga.
Website: www.seaisland.com
Teaching since: 1958
Top 100 since: 1996

RON GRING
Facility: Gring Golf, Daphne, Ala.
Website: www.gringgolf.com
Teaching since: 1978
Top 100 since: 2003
See Ron's tips on page 11

HANK JOHNSON
Facility: Greystone G.C., Birmingham, Ala.
Website: www.greystonecc.com
Teaching since: 1969
Top 100 since: 1999

KEITH LYFORD
Facility: Auburn C.C., Auburn, Calif.
Website: www.lyfordgolf.cnet
Teaching since: 1982
Top 100 since: 1999
See Keith's tips on page 81

ROGER GUNN
Facility: Tierra Rejada G.C., Moorpark, Calif.
Website: www.golflevels.com
Teaching since: 1993
Top 100 since: 2007
See Roger's tips on page 32

DARRELL KESTNER
Facility: Deepdale G.C., Manhasset, N.Y.
Website: www.deepdalegolfclub.com
Teaching since: 1980
Top 100 since: 1996
See Darrell's tips on pages 34, 37, 101 and 136

BILL MADONNA
Facility: Bill Madonna G.A, Orlando, Fla.
Website: www.marriottworldcenter.com
Teaching since: 1971
Top 100 since: 1996
See Bill's tips on pages 23 and 55

MARTIN HALL
Facility: Ibis Golf & C.C., West Palm Beach, Fla.
Website: www.ibisgolf.com
Teaching since: 1978
Top 100 since: 1996
See Martin's tips on pages 30, 32, 57, 60, 65, 137 and 138

CHARLIE KING
Facility: Reynolds Plantation, Greensboro, Ga.
Website: www.reynoldsgolfacademy.com
Teaching since: 1989
Top 100 since: 2003
See Charlie's tips on page 39

TIM MAHONEY
Facility: Talking Stick G.C., Scottsdale, Ariz.
Website: www.timmahoneygolf.com
Teaching since: 1980
Top 100 since: 1996
See Tim's tips on page 34, 57, 68, 71 and 97

BRUCE HAMILTON
Facility: Spanish Hills C.C., Camarillo, Calif.
Website: www.spanishhills.com
Teaching since: 1973
Top 100 since: 1996
See Bruce's tips on page 33

PETER KOSTIS
Facility: Kostis/McCord Learning Center, Scottsdale, Ariz.
Website: www.kostismccordlearning.com
Teaching since: 1971
Top 100 since: 1996
See Peter's tips on page 63

MIKE MALASKA
Facility: Superstition Mtn. G. & C.C., Superstition Mtn., Ariz.
Website: www.malaskagolf.com
Teaching since: 1982
Top 100 since: 1996
See Mike's tips on pages 48, 49 and 55

HANK HANEY
Facility: Hank Haney Golf Ranch, McKinney, Tex.
Website: www.hankhaney.com
Teaching since: 1977
Top 100 since: 1996

DON KOTNIK
Facility: Toledo Country Club, Toledo, Ohio
Website: www.toledocountryclub.com
Teaching since: 1969
Top 100 since: 2005
See Don's tips on page 82

PAUL MARCHAND
Facility: Shadow Hawk G.C., Richmond, Tex.
Website: www.golfspan.com
Teaching since: 1981
Top 100 since: 1996
See Paul's tips on page 105

JIM HARDY
Facility: Jim Hardy Golf, Houston, Tex.
Website: www.jimhardygolf.com
Teaching since: 1966
Top 100 since: 1996
See Jim's tips on page 12

PETER KRAUSE
Facility: Windsong Farm G.C., Independence, Minn.
Website: www.peterkrausegolf.com
Teaching since: 1981
Top 100 since: 1999
See Peter's tips on page 7

LYNN MARRIOTT
Facility: Legacy Golf Resort, Phoenix, Ariz.
Website: www.golf54.com
Teaching since: 1982
Top 100 since: 1996
See Lynn's tips on page 119

BUTCH HARMON, JR.
Facility: Butch Harmon School of Golf, Henderson, Nev.
Website: www.butchharmon.com
Teaching since: 1965
Top 100 since: 1996

MIKE LaBAUVE
Facility: Westin Kierland Resort and Spa, Scottsdale, Ariz.
Website: www.kierlandresort.com
Teaching since: 1980
Top 100 since: 1996
See Mike's tips on pages 50, 51 and 85

RICK MARTINO
Facility: PGA Village, Port St. Lucie, Fla.
Website: www.pgavillage.com
Teaching since: 1970
Top 100 since: 2003
See Rick's tips on page 57

CONTRIBUTORS

RICK McCORD
Facility: McCord G.A. at Orange Lake Resort, Kissimmee, Fla.
Website: www.themccordgolfacademy.com
Teaching since: 1973
Top 100 since: 1996
See Rick's tips on pages 14, 64, 94 and 95

GERALD McCULLAGH
Facility: Univ. of Minn. Le Bolstad G.C., Falcon Heights, Minn.
Website: www.uofmgolf.com
Teaching since: 1967
Top 100 since: 1996
See Gerald's tips on page 11

MIKE McGETRICK
Facility: Mike McGetrick G.A., Denver, Colo.
Website: www.mcgetrickgolf.com
Teaching since: 1983
Top 100 since: 1996

PATTI McGOWAN
Facility: Knack 4 Golf, Orlando, Fla.
Website: www.knack4golf.com
Teaching since: 1986
Top 100 since: 1996
See Patti's tips on page 131

JIM McLEAN
Facility: Jim McLean G.S. at Doral Golf Resort, Miami, Fla.
Website: www.jimmclean.com
Teaching since: 1975
Top 100 since: 1996

BRIAN MOGG
Facility: Golden Bear G.C. at Keene's Pointe, Windermere, Fla.
Website: www.moggperformance.com
Teaching since: 1992
Top 100 since: 2005
See Brian's tips on pages 19, 29, 64, 89 and 99

BILL MORETTI
Facility: Academy of Golf Dynamics, Austin, Tex.
Website: www.golfdynamics.com
Teaching since: 1979
Top 100 since: 1996
See Bill's tips on pages 96 and 131

JERRY MOWLDS
Facility: Pumpkin Ridge G.C., North Plains, Or.
Website: www.pumpkinridge.com
Teaching since: 1970
Top 100 since: 1996
See Jerry's tips on pages 77 and 109

JIM MURPHY
Facility: Sugar Creek C.C., Sugar Land, Tex.
Website: www.jimmurphygolf.com
Teaching since: 1984
Top 100 since: 2003
See Jim's tips on pages 62 and 91

TOM NESS
Facility: Golf Academy at Chateau Elan Resort, Braselton, Ga.
Website: www.chateauelanatlanta.com
Teaching since: 1972
Top 100 since: 2007

PIA NILSSON
Facility: Legacy Golf Resort, Phoenix, Ariz.
Website: www.golf54.com
Teaching since: 1987
Top 100 since: 2001
See Pia's tips on page 44

DAN PASQUARIELLO
Facility: Pebble Beach G.A., Pebble Beach, Calif.
Website: www.pebblebeach.com
Teaching since: 1970
Top 100 since: 2007
See Dan's tips on page 44

TOM PATRI
Facility: Friar's Head G.C., Baiting Hollow, N.Y.
Website: www.tompatri.com
Teaching since: 1981
Top 100 since: 2001
See Tom's tips on page 114

BRUCE PATTERSON
Facility: Butler National G.C., Oak Brook, Ill.
Website: None
Teaching since: 1980
Top 100 since: 2005
See Bruce's tips on page 7

MIKE PERPICH
Facility: RiverPines Golf, Alpharetta, Ga.
Website: www.mikeperpich.com
Teaching since: 1976
Top 100 since: 2001
See Mike's tips on page 64

GALE PETERSON
Facility: Sea Island Golf Learning Ctr., St. Simons Island, Ga.
Website: www.seaisland.com
Teaching since: 1978
Top 100 since: 1996
See Mike's tips on page 11

DAVID PHILLIPS
Facility: Titleist Performance Institute, Oceanside, Calif.
Website: www.titleistperformanceinstitute.com
Teaching since: 1989
Top 100 since: 2001
See David's tips on pages 9 and 15

CAROL PREISINGER
Facility: Kiawah Island Club G.A., Kiawah Island, S.C.
Website: www.kiawahislandclub.com
Teaching since: 1986
Top 100 since: 2005
See Carol's tips on pages 15, 71 and 139

KIP PUTERBAUGH
Facility: The Aviara G.A., Carlsbad, Calif.
Website: www.aviaragolfacademy.com
Teaching since: 1972
Top 100 since: 1996
See Kip's tips on pages 76 and 77

NANCY QUARCELINO
Facility: King's Creek G.C., Spring Hill, Tenn.
Website: www.qsog.com
Teaching since: 1979
Top 100 since: 2003
See Nancy's tips on page 22

CARL RABITO
Facility: Rabito Golf at Bolingbrook G.C., Bolingbrook, Ill.
Website: www.rabitogolf.com
Teaching since: 1987
Top 100 since: 2007
See Carl's tips on page 31

DANA RADER
Facility: Ballantyne Resort, Charlotte, N.C.
Website: www.danarader.com
Teaching since: 1980
Top 100 since: 1996
See Dana's tips on page 37

BRAD REDDING
Facility: The Resort Club at Grande Dunes, Myrtle Beach, S.C.
Website: www.bradreddinggolf.com
Teaching since: 1984
Top 100 since: 2001
See Brad's tips on page 136

DEIN REINMUTH
Facility: Dean Reinmuth G.S., San Diego, Calif.
Website: www.deanofgolf.com
Teaching since: 1978
Top 100 since: 1996

BRADY RIGGS
Facility: Woodley Lakes G.C., Van Nuys, Calif.
Website: www.bradyriggs.com
Teaching since: 1990
Top 100 since: 2007
See Brady's tips on page 33

SCOTT SACKETT
Facility: PGA Tour G.A., St. Augustine, Fla.
Website: www.scottsackett.com
Teaching since: 1985
Top 100 since: 1999
See Scott's tips on pages 30, 104, 105 and 117

TED SHEFTIC
Facility: Bridges G.C., Abbottstown, Pa.
Website: www.tedsheftic.com
Teaching since: 1966
Top 100 since: 2003
See Ted's tips on page 63

LAIRD SMALL
Facility: Pebble Beach G.A., Pebble Beach, Calif.
Website: www.pebblebeach.com
Teaching since: 1977
Top 100 since: 1996
See Laird's tips on pages 40, 41, 134 and 135

RANDY SMITH
Facility: Royal Oaks C.C., Dallas, Tex.
Website: www.roccdallas.com
Teaching since: 1973
Top 100 since: 2001

RICK SMITH
Facility: Rick Smith Golf Academy at Tiburon, Naples, Fla.
Website: www.ricksmith.com
Teaching since: 1977
Top 100 since: 1996

TODD SONES
Facility: White Deer Run G.C., Vernon Hills, Ill.
Website: www.toddsones.com
Teaching since: 1982
Top 100 since: 1996
See Todd's tips on pages 56, 57, 86, 87, 107 and 118

CHARLES SORRELL
Facility: Sorrell School of Golf, Stockbridge, Ga.
Website: www.sorrellgolf.com
Teaching since: 1966
Top 100 since: 1996
See Charles' tips on page 80

MITCHELL SPEARMAN
Facility: Manhattan Woods G.C., West Nyack, N.Y.
Website: www.mitchellspearman.com
Teaching since: 1979
Top 100 since: 1996
See Mitchell's tips on page 23

TOM F. STICKNEY II
Facility: The Club at Cordillera, Edwards, Colo.
Website: www.tomstickneygolf.com
Teaching since: 1990
Top 100 since: 2007
See Tom's tips on pages 129 and 137

EMERITUS
The master class of the Top 100 Teachers in America provide over a half-millennium's worth of instruction know-how

JON TATTERSALL
Facility: Golf Performance Partners, Atlanta, Ga.
Website: www.golfpp.com
Teaching since: 1986
Top 100 since: 2007
See Jon's tips on pages 28 and 64

JIMMY BALLARD
Facility: Ballard Swing Connection, Key Largo, Fla.
Website: www.jimmyballard.com
Teaching since: 1960
Top 100 since: 1996
See Mr. Ballard's tips on page 60

PHIL RODGERS
Facility: Carlton Oaks C.C., San Diego, Calif.
Website: None
Teaching since: 1977
Top 100 since: 1996

DR. T.J. TOMASI
Facility: Nantucket G.C., Siasconset, Mass.
Website: www.tjtomasi.com
Teaching since: 1975
Top 100 since: 1999
See T.J.'s tips on page 17

PEGGY KIRK BELL
Facility: Pine Needles Resort, Southern Pines, N.C.
Website: www.pineneedles-midpines.com
Teaching since: 1958
Top 100 since: 1996
See Ms. Kirk Bell's tips on page 32

CRAIG SHANKLAND
Facility: Craig Shankland G.S., Daytona Beach, Fla.
Website: None
Teaching since: 1957
Top 100 since: 1996
See Mr. Shankland's tips on page 54

PAUL TRITTLER
Facility: Kostis/McCord Learning Ctr., Scottsdale, Ariz.
Website: www.kostismccordlearning.com
Teaching since: 1983
Top 100 since: 1999
See Paul's tips on pages 65, 110 and 111

CHUCK COOK
Facility: Chuck Cook G.A. at Barton Creek C.C., Austin, Tex.
Website: www.bartoncreek.com
Teaching since: 1975
Top 100 since: 1996

DR. JIM SUTTIE
Facility: Suttie Academies at TwinEagles, Naples, Fla.
Website: www.jimsuttie.com
Teaching since: 1972
Top 100 since: 1996
See Dr. Suttie's tips on pages 103 and 116

J.D. TURNER
Facility: The Turner Golf Group, Savannah, Ga.
Website: www.jdturnergolf.com
Teaching since: 1965
Top 100 since: 1996
See J.D.'s tips on page 79

MANUEL DE LA TORRE
Facility: Milwaukee C.C., River Hills, Wis.
Website: www.manueldelatorregolf.com
Teaching since: 1948
Top 100 since: 1996
See Mr. de la Torre's tips on page 75

BOB TOSKI
Facility: Toski-Battersby Golf Learning Ctr., Coconut Creek, Fla.
Website: www.learn-golf.com
Teaching since: 1956
Top 100 since: 1996
See Mr. Toski's tips on page 19

KEVIN WALKER
Facility: Nantucket G.C., Siasconset, Mass.
Website: None
Teaching since: 1979
Top 100 since: 1996
See Kevin's tips on pages 22 and 35

JIM FLICK
Facility: Jim Flick Golf, Carlsbad, Calif.
Website: www.jimflick.com
Teaching since: 1954
Top 100 since: 1996

DR. GARY WIREN
Facility: Trump International G.C., West Palm Beach, Fla.
Website: www.garywiren.com
Teaching since: 1955
Top 100 since: 1996
See Dr. Wiren's tips on pages 109, 122 and 128

CARL WELTY, JR.
Facility: Jim McLean G.S. at PGA West, La Quinta, Calif.
Website: www.jimmclean.com/usa/pga-west
Teaching since: 1965
Top 100 since: 1996
See Carl's tips on page 15

MICHAEL HEBRON
Facility: Smithtown Landing G.C., Smithtown, N.Y.
Website: www.mikehebron.com
Teaching since: 1967
Top 100 since: 1996
See Mr. Hebron's tips on page 28

CHUCK WINSTEAD
Facility: The University Club, Baton Rouge, La.
Website: www.universityclubbr.com
Teaching since: 1993
Top 100 since: 2005
See Chuck's tips on page 115

DAVID LEADBETTER
Facility: David Leadbetter G.A, Champions Gate, Fla.
Website: www.davidleadbetter.com
Teaching since: 1976
Top 100 since: 1996

29.23
Average years of teaching experience

20
Top 100 Teachers who have been named PGA National Teacher of the Year

MARK WOOD
Facility: Cornerstone Club, Montrose, Colo.
Website: www.cornerstonecolorado.com
Teaching since: 1984
Top 100 since: 1999
See Mark's tips on page 123

EDDIE MERRINS
Facility: Bel-Air C.C., Los Angeles, Calif.
Website: www.eddiemerrins.com
Teaching since: 1957
Top 100 since: 1996
See Mr. Merrin's tips on page 116

6
Top 100 Teachers who have been inducted into the PGA Golf Professional Hall of Fame

DR. DAVID WRIGHT
Facility: Arroyo Trabuco Golf Club
Website: www.wrightbalance.com
Teaching since: 1982
Top 100 since: 2005
See David's tips on pages 17, 23 and 83

DAVE PELZ
Facility: Dave Pelz Scoring Game School, Austin, Tex.
Website: www.pelzgolf.com
Teaching since: 1976
Top 100 since: 1996
See Mr. Pelz's tips on pages 8, 9, 82, 111 and 119

28,000
Members of the PGA of America's 41 sections eligible for Top 100 Status

Get more information on GOLF Magazine's Top 100 Teachers and the Top Teachers by Region, plus exclusive video tips and drills at **GOLF.com**

PHIL RITSON
Facility: Orange County National, Winter Garden, Fla.
Website: www.ocngolf.com
Teaching since: 1950
Top 100 since: 1996
See Mr. Ritson's tips on page 61

0.4%
Percentage of those who are Top 100 Teachers

BOOK DESIGN

PAUL EWEN

PHOTOGRAPHY

BOB ATKINS: 9, 16-17, 22 (R), 33 (T), 40, 41 (L), 44, 46, 47 (L), 50, 51, 55 (R), 57 (M), 59 (BR), 60, 61 (B), 65 (M), 66-67, 79 (B), 81 (BR), 83, 91 (T), 93 (T), 98, 99 (L), 101 (TR, BR), 102-103, 105 (M), 109 (R), 112-113, 115, 119 (BR), 120, 121, 124-125, 134, 135

NEIL BECKERMAN: 35 (R), 72, 73

D2 PRODUCTIONS: 74-75, 92, 106, 117 (B), 126-127

SAM GREENWOOD: 22 (L), 37 (BL), 54 (TR), 57 (BL), 79 (T), 105 (B), 123 (BR), 138

LEONARD KAMSLER: 8, 12, 21, 23, 24, 25, 31 (L), 38, 39, 54 (L), 55 (BL), 61 (T), 65 (BR), 68 (R), 71 (M), 81 (TR), 82, 91 (B), 114, 119 (T, BL)

RUSSELL KIRK: 54 (BR), 56, 57 (T), 62, 63 (B), 139

SCHECTER LEE: 4, 35 (L), 88, 105 (TR)

GREG LORD: 13, 67 (BL)

ANGUS MURRAY:
1, 2-3, 6-7, 10, 11, 14, 18, 19, 20 (R), 26, 27, 28, 30, 31 (R), 32, 33 (B), 34 (B), 36, 37 (TL, BR), 41 (R), 42, 43, 45, 47 (BR), 48, 49, 52-53, 58-59, 64, 65 (L), 69, 70, 71 (L), 78, 84-85, 86, 87, 89, 93 (B), 94, 95, 97, 99 (R), 100, 101 (L), 107, 108, 109 (L), 116, 117 (T), 118, 122, 123 (T, BR), 128, 129, 130, 132-133, 136, 137

GARY NEWKIRK: 76, 77, 110, 111

KEICHI SATO: 169 (BR)

FRED VUICH:
20 (L), 29, 34 (T), 37 (TR), 57 (BR), 63 (T), 68 (L), 71 (BR), 90, 96, 104, 131 (L)

ILLUSTRATIONS

KEVIN BEARD: 15, 17, 53, 64, 73, 75, 99, 103, 125

PHIL FRANKE: 96, 118

ROBIN GRIGGS: 23, 39, 51, 80-81, 121

KAREN HA: 61, 135

PETE SUCHESKI: 83

IAN WARPOLE: 105

THANK YOU

Alan Bastable, Kevin Beard, Steve Beslow, Glenn Buonocore, Dr. Richard Coop, Caroline DeOliveira, Noelle Ewen, Margaret Hess, Suzanne Janso, Robert Marasco, Dennis Marcel, Jess Marksbury, Holly Oakes, Patrice Peelen-Wenz, Brooke Reger, Jesse Reiter, Josh Sanburn, Mary Sarro-Waite, Rob Sauerhaft, Roger Sauerhaft, Ilene Schreider, Lisa Taddeo, Adriana Tierno, Alex Voznesenskiy, Kris Widger, Ken Yagoda

CHARLIE HANGER Executive Editor
DAVID DUSEK Deputy Editor
RYAN REITERMAN, ANNE SZEKER Producers
OMAR SHARIF Associate Art Director

RICHARD FRAIMAN Publisher
STEVEN SANDONATO General Manager
CAROL PITTARD Executive Director, Marketing Services
TOM MIFSUD Director, Retail & Special Sales
PETER HARPER Director, New Product Development
LAURA ADAM Assistant Director, Brand Marketing
HELEN WAN General Counsel
SUSAN CHODAKIEWICZ Book Production Manager
ANNE-MICHELLE GALLERO Design & Prepress Manager
ALEXANDRA BLISS Marketing Manager

DAVID M. CLARKE Editor
PAUL CRAWFORD Creative Director
MICHAEL CORCORAN Deputy Editor
DAVID DeNUNZIO Managing Editor (Instruction)
EAMON LYNCH Content Development Editor
CONNELL BARRETT Editor At Large
MICHAEL WALKER, JR. Senior Editor
GARY PERKINSON Production Editor
PAUL EWEN Art Director
KAREN HA Deputy Art Director
CARRIE BORETZ Photo Editor
CHARLES R. KAMMERER Publisher
NATHAN STAMOS Associate Publisher
BRAD J. FELENSTEIN Director of Business Development
PETER GREER General Manager
BILL KEATING National Director of Online Sales
MIKE WYWODA Vice President of Consumer Marketing

MARK FORD President/Publisher
TERRY McDONELL Editor
OLIVER KNOWLTON Vice President, General Manager
JEFF PRICE President, SI Digital
DAVID BAUER Deputy Managing Editor
MICHAEL BEVANS, CHARLIE LEERHSEN Executive Editors
ANDREW R. JUDELSON Chief Marketing Officer
RICHARD A. RASKOPF Associate Publisher
NEIL COHEN, JAMES HERRE, CRAIG NEFF
Asst. Managing Editors